The Sims superstar

Prima's Official Strategy Guide

Mark Cohen

Prima Games
A Division of Random House, Inc.

3000 Lava Ridge Court
Roseville, CA 95661
1-800-733-3000
www.primagames.com

Prima's Official Strategy Guide

Associate Product Manager: Christy L. Curtis
Project Editor: Teli Hernandez

A very special thanks to Jonathan Knight: Producer, Vicki Fairchild: Software Engineer, Jenna Chalmers: Associate Designer, Charles Gast: Software Engineer, Waylon Wilsonoff: Assistant Producer, Juan Custer: Software Engineer, Cooper Buckingham: Assistant Producer; and last but certainly not least, Jeannie Wang, Assistant Producer, who fielded a barrage of questions and requests, while maintaining a high Social Motive.

ISBN: 0-7615-4322-8
Library of Congress Catalog Card Number: 2003104844
Printed in the United States of America

03 04 05 06 DD 10 9 8 7 6 5 4 3 2 1

Introduction

After years of dating, partying, vacationing, and dog training, the time has come to get serious about your career. *Sims Superstar* is the first expansion pack to follow you from the house to your job, spanning a vast new neighborhood called Studio Town, a glittery entertainment mecca with nine all-new Community Lots. You ride the car pool to your first gig in Studio Town, and if you play your cards right, you drive home in a pink limousine, just in time to give your Butler his instructions for an evening party.

But don't make the mistake of thinking this is a studio tour ride. The road from Nobody to Superstar is paved with broken dreams, and only a few celebrities make it to the coveted "Who's Hot in Studio Town?" list. You must develop your talents as actor, singer, and model, and if you make the right friends (and step on the right people), you might make it to the top.

Sims Superstar introduces over 120 new items, including nine unique Community Lots, at which your Sim performs for producers, directors, and finicky clothing designers. At home, find new luxury objects befitting an up-and-coming celebrity, such as a full-size Scuba Tank, Skydiving Simulator, and Oxygen Bar.

This guide covers the many new features of *Sims Superstar*, including a glossary of objects, complete Fame tutorial, and detailed strategies managing your Sim's career. After selling millions of copies, *The Sims* still attracts new converts every day, so we also cover the original game, with detailed interaction tables and complete tutorials on all aspects of Sim life. So whether you're a veteran or a newbie, everything you need to find happiness and fulfillment as a Sim lies in these pages. The following previews what you find in this guide.

Part I: The Sims

The first part takes you on a detailed tour through the original *Sims* game. We explain how a Sim thinks, acts, and reacts in various situations; and we teach you how to select and blend your Sim's personality traits. Next comes the Motives, the eight primal urges that drive all Sims. We cover each Motive in detail and show how to manipulate your Sim's world to create happiness and contentment.

Sims are very social creatures, which can be a blessing or a curse. We demonstrate how and why a Sim interacts with others and explain the benefits and pitfalls that accompany every short-term and long-term relationship. If your Sim's future includes marriage and children, find out what to expect when the blessed day arrives.

Sims spend simoleans at a staggering rate, so you must think about a job and a successful career. We cover all the career paths, with extensive tables detailing salaries, work schedules and promotion requirements.

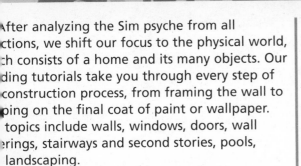

After analyzing the Sim psyche from all ctions, we shift our focus to the physical world, ch consists of a home and its many objects. Our ding tutorials take you through every step of construction process, from framing the wall to ping on the final coat of paint or wallpaper. topics include walls, windows, doors, wall erings, stairways and second stories, pools, landscaping.

A Sim home is empty until you fill it with stuff, we provide facts and statistics on every object can buy—over 120 items in all. In addition to a and descriptions, we use detailed lists and es to show how items relate to one another how some objects can alter the effectiveness thers.

rt 2: Sims Superstar

begin the second section of our guide with lcome to Studio Town," including a tour of following all-new Community Lots:

WLW Studios

irchild Film Studios

eeker Studios

idlock Multiplex

udio Town Center

uckingham Galleries

usic For the Eyes, Inc.

ameron's Lounge

he Gast District

Next, we delve inside the complex Fame career. The **"Almost Famous"** and **"Art of Schmoozing"** sections include tips and strategies for all ten career levels. We explain how *Sims Superstar* calculates Starpower, offer strategies for developing Famous Friends, teach you how to deal with Obsessed Fans, and show you how to keep your Sim from having a Nervous Breakdown.

In **"Lights, Camera, Action!"** we take you through an entire career, from the Karaoke Stage to the Movie Set. Finally, the **"New Objects"** section includes pictures and data for over 120 new objects, providing easy reference to the necessities of a celebrity lifestyle.

There you have it—everything you need to transform your Sim from an off-key Karaoke crooner to the highest paid entertainer in Studio Town. In *Sims Superstar* all that glitters really is gold—if you possess the stuff that stars are made of!

PART 1:

The SIMS™

CHAPTER 1:
WHAT'S YOUR SIM SIGN?

troduction

en you are charged with the solemn task of
ting a Sim from scratch, you have 25 points to
ribute over five traits: Neat, Outgoing, Active,
ful, and Nice. Whether we admit it or not, all
s have an inherent wish to be perfectly
nced people (or Sims). Of course, you can take
easy way out and award five points in every
gory, creating a generic Sim. You'll spend less
managing a middle-of-the-road Sim because
ost situations, he or she will do the right
g. If you'd rather play it safe, skip this chapter
move right to "Motives: I Want, I Need;
efore, I Am a Sim." If not, read on as we
ribe the subtle (and sometimes dramatic)
comes that your Sim's personality ratings
inspire.

s in the Stars

ou play with the personality bars, you'll note
changing zodiac sign that appears on the
en. Of course, a serious astrologer would argue
t a true personality profile is based on much
re than five traits. However, if you have a basic
erstanding of newspaper horoscopes, you'll be
to recognize yourself, or someone close to
, as you create a Sim personality. In the next
ion we'll look at each trait and examine the
ential effects of your ratings in various game
ations. But first, let's take a look at basic
erpersonal compatibility as seen through the
s of the zodiac. The following table gives you
best and worst matchups for friends and
ers. This doesn't necessarily imply that any other
ationship outside of the table is doomed; it is
rely an indication of how hard you'll have to
rk on it.

Sims Zodiac Compatibility Table

SIGN	ATTRACTED TO	REPELLED BY
Aries	Gemini/Taurus	Cancer/Libra
Taurus	Aries/Libra	Virgo/Cancer
Gemini	Pisces/Virgo	Capricorn/Aries
Cancer	Taurus/Scorpio	Gemini/Aries
Virgo	Aquarius/Sagittarius	Leo/Taurus
Libra	Virgo/Cancer	Pisces/Scorpio
Scorpio	Pisces/Leo	Libra/Aquarius
Sagittarius	Pisces/Capricorn	Libra/Scorpio
Leo	Sagittarius/Cancer	Capricorn/Gemini
Capricorn	Aquarius/Taurus	Leo/Gemini
Aquarius	Capricorn/Sagittarius	Scorpio/Virgo
Pisces	Scorpio/Gemini	Leo/Aries

Personality Traits

The following sections review what you can
expect from each type of Sim, with examples of
how different personality traits will manifest
during the game. For our purposes, we'll divide
the ratings bar into three sections: Low (1–3),
Average (4–7), and High (8–10). These numbers
correspond to the number of light blue bars to
the right of each trait.

Neat

Low

Don't expect these Sims to pick up their dirty
dishes, wash their hands after using the bathroom,
or take timely showers. They are perfectly content
to let others clean up their messes.

Fig. 1-1. The kitchen floor is a perfect place for this messy Sim's snack leavings.

Fig. 1-3. This fastidious Sim straight to the bathtub after hard day's wor

Medium

At least these Sims keep themselves relatively clean, and you can depend on them to clean up their own messes. Occasionally, they'll even clean up another Sim's garbage, but you might have to intervene if you have several cleanup items that need attention.

Fig. 1-2. After slopping water all over the bathroom during his shower, this moderately Neat Sim mops up his mess before leaving the room.

High

A super-Neat Sim always checks the vicinity for dirty dishes and old newspapers, and of course, personal hygiene is a big priority. One of these Sims can compensate for one or two slobs in a household.

Outgoing

Low

Shy, reserved, Sims have less pressing needs for Social interaction, so it will be more difficult to pursue friendships with other Sims, although the can still carry on stimulating conversations. With their own home, a shy Sim may be less interested receiving hugs, kisses, and back rubs, so if you ar looking for romance, it would be a good idea to find a compatible target (see zodiac chart on p.

Fig. 1-4. This Si cringes at the thought of a ba rub—poor guy.

dium

ll be a little easier to get this Sim to mix with
ngers and enjoy a little intimacy from his
semates. Don't expect a party animal, but you'll
ble to entice your guests into most activities.

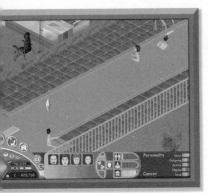

Fig. 1-5. Come on everyone, let's hit the pool!

h

Sim needs plenty of Social stimulation to
vent his or her Social score from plummeting.
'll have no trouble throwing parties or breaking
ice with just about any personality type.

Fig. 1-6. This outgoing Sim is still unconscious from last night's pool party, and she has inspired the close friendship of another man. Hmmm.

Active

Low

Forget about pumping iron or swimming 100
laps at 5:00 a.m. These Sims prefer a soft easy
chair to a hard workout. A sofa and a good TV
are high on their priority list. In fact, if they
don't get their daily ration of vegging, their
Comfort scores will suffer.

Fig. 1-7. This Sim says "No way!" to a session on the exercise bench.

Medium

These Sims strike a good balance between relaxing
and breaking a sweat. They dance, swim, and even
shoot hoops without expressing discomfort.

Fig. 1-8. His Active rating is only a four, but that doesn't stop this Sim from shooting hoops in his jammies.

High

Active Sims like to pick up the pace rather than fall asleep on the sofa in front of the TV. Get these Sims a pool, basketball hoop, or exercise bench, and plan on dancing the night away with friends.

Fig. 1-9. Even in her business suit, this active Sim will gladly leave Mortimer on the sofa and pump some iron in the backyard.

Medium

These well-rounded Sims are usually receptive t◦ good joke and don't mind a little tickling. They may not be the first ones on the dance floor, bu they'll join in with a good crowd.

Fig. 1-11. This Playful enough dance, even th◦ she is overdue a shower.

Playful

Low

Get these Sims a bookcase, a comfortable chair, and plenty of books. If reading isn't an option, looking at a painting or playing a game of chess will do just fine.

Fig. 1-10. There's always time to watch the fish, for this less-than-playful Sim.

High

Can you spell P-A-R-T-Y? These Sims love to hav a few drinks, dance to good music, and invite l◦ of guests over to the house. They love telling jokes, and they are usually ready to laugh at others' stories.

Fig. 1-12. This Playful kid wou◦ get the Maid in pool for a game chicken, if only would respond.

Fig. 1-15. Even after spending the night on the kitchen floor, this Sim still knows how to compliment her mate.

e is nothing redeeming about a grouchy Sim.
are always ready to tease or insult their friends,
they love to brag. A Sim with a low Nice rating
ld be dropped from your guest list immediately,
ked to leave if he or she shows up.

Fig. 1-13. Usually a compliment elicits a nice response, but not so with with sourpuss.

ium

Sim keeps an even keel about most things. Of
he traits, Nice is the least destructive if you
rd at least four points. Only the nastiest Sims
get under a medium-Nice Sim's skin.

Fig. 1-14. This Sim has time for a good tickle, even while mopping up the bathroom.

h

se Sims just want to make the world a better
e for everyone. If there was a Sim beauty
test, the winner would be extremely "Nice."

Personality Tables

The following tables demonstrate how personality traits affect Fun scores and Skill development.

Traits that Raise Max Fun Value

PERSONALITY TRAIT	RAISES MAX FUN SCORE FOR
Playful	Aquarium, Chess Table, Computer, Doll House, Flamingo, Pinball, TV (Cartoon Channel), VR Glasses
Serious (Low Playful)	Newspaper (Read)
Active	Basketball Hoop, Play Structure, TV (Action Channel)
Outgoing	Hot Tub, TV (Romance Channel)
Grouchy (Low Nice)	TV (Horror Channel)

Skills Accelerated by Personality

SKILL	OBJECTS USED TO INCREASE SKILL	TRAIT ACCELERATOR
Creativity	Easel, Piano	Playful
Body	Exercise Machine, Swimming Pool	Active
Charisma	Medicine Cabinet, Mirrors	Outgoing

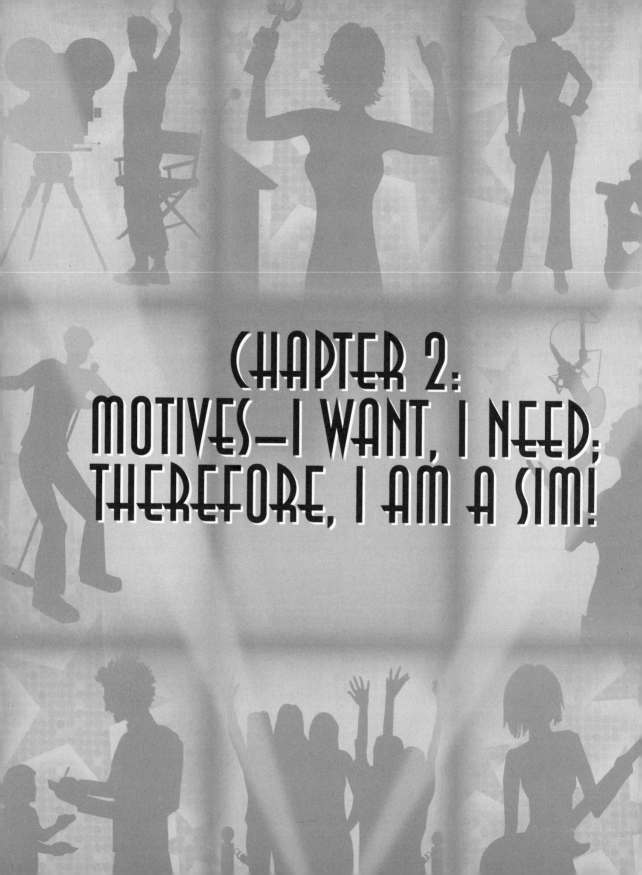

CHAPTER 2:
MOTIVES—I WANT, I NEED; THEREFORE, I AM A SIM!

Introduction

When you consider how many needs, traits, and desires make up a Sim's personality, it would be an injustice to call it AI. Never before has a computer-generated character interacted so completely with both the game and the gamer while maintaining a unique (and ever-changing) personality. Is it any wonder that *The Sims* has topped the PC sales chart for nearly two years running?

In the previous chapter we discussed a Sim's personality traits. It painted a broad picture of the various types of Sims you might encounter in the game, much the same as a newspaper horoscope tells a superficial story of a person's life. In this chapter, we advance from broad-brush personality traits to the eight powerful Motives that drive a Sim's every action. We cover each Motive in detail, but first, let's begin with a few basic definitions.

What Is a Motive?

A Motive is, very simply, a need. Your Sims follow these needs, based on their own instincts and a little help from you. If you activate Free Will in the Options menu, your Sims will also make their own decisions, based on changing needs. After selecting a Motive to fulfill, be it Hunger or Hygiene, the Sim is "rewarded" with Motive points. These points raise the corresponding Motive score.

The eight Motive scores are displayed on the right side of the control panel. A Motive rating is considered positive if the bar is green, and negative if it is red. Internally, the game uses a 200-point system, with positive (green) ratings between 0 and 100, and negative (red) ratings from 0 to -100.

> **TIP** When any of the Sims' eight Motives drop below a certain level, a Sim will cease an activity that doesn't improve the Motive in distress. So, you'll see low-priority items drop out of the activity queue, or your Sim will add an activity that addresses the critical need.

> **CAUTION**
> *Without Free Will, your Sims depend entirely on your input to keep them alive. If you don't tell them to eat, they will starve, and eventually die.*

Mood Rating

The game control panel also displays a Mood Rating, just to the right of the Sim character icons. If the rating is positive, you see up to five green bars displayed above the comedy/tragedy masks. When the Mood Rating is negative, it displays up to five red bars below the masks.

In calculating the Mood Rating, each of the eight Motives is weighted, based on how critical it is to sustaining a Sim's life. Hence, Hunger, Bladder, and Energy, which are all related to a Sim's physical well-being, carry more weight than the noncritical Motives such as Social, Fun, or Room. So, if a Sim is hungry and tired, as pictured in figure 2-1, the overall Mood Rating will be relatively low, even if several other Motives are high.

Fig. 2-1. This Sim kid's overall Mood Rating is barely positive, due to the fact that he is starving and low on Energy.

The Motives

In the following sections we describe the eight Motives, using several tables to show you how and why a Sim reacts to different objects in the environment. By recognizing the relationships between Motives and objects, you'll begin to understand how a Sim considers a perpetual barrage of options. Once you do this, the only remaining question is, "Who is really in charge here, you or the Sim?"

Fig. 2-2. This Sim family enjoys a meal together. Mom's Hunger ba is in the worst shape, so she has second meal plat at the ready.

> ## NOTE
>
> *Aside from the overall Motive weighting system, each Sim suffers different rates of Motive depreciation based on personality traits. For example, a Playful Sim must have more "rewards" to maintain the Fun Motive bar. Similarly, an Outgoing Sim requires more interaction with other Sims to maintain the Social score.*

Hunger Score for Each Meal, Snack, or Gift

MEAL TYPE	HUNGER MOTIVE BAR POINT
Snack	9
Quick Meal	16
Full Meal	16
Group Meal (per serving)	16
Pizza (per serving)	33
Candy Box (gift)	3 (per serving, 12 servings per box)
Fruitcake (gift)	7 (per slice, 6 slices per box)

Hunger

For obvious reasons, a Sim cannot survive for very long without food. We'll cover the details of food preparation in a later chapter, but for now let's focus on the basics. As long as you have a refrigerator, a Sim can enjoy a Snack, Quick Meal, Full Meal, or Group Meal (same as a Full Meal, except one of the Sims prepares several servings). In addition to preparing food, a Sim with a telephone can order out for Pizza, or enjoy food that was brought as a gift (Candy Box or Fruitcake). The Hunger Motive bar points awarded with each meal are outlined in the following table.

Comfort

The next category listed in the Needs section of the control panel is considerably less important than Hunger. Sims like to be comfortable, and th love cushy chairs, oversized sofas, and supportive beds. Spending more money on these objects translates into greater Motive rewards. However, your budget is tight, you must still furnish the house with basic furniture or your Sims will expr their discomfort.

Fig. 2-3. With only a cheap chair and loveseat, this Sim's Comfort score is mired in the red.

Fig. 2-4. Three out of four Motive scores are on the way up while this couple enjoys a hot tub soak.

...unger, Bladder, Energy, and Comfort are the ...ost demanding of Motives, because if any one ...ore drops below a certain level, the Sim will ...mmediately exit his or her current activity to ...emedy the deficit. The following table lists the ...xit triggers for each category.

Mandatory Exit Factors

MOTIVE	SIM TYPE	EXITS CURRENT INTERACTION WHEN MOTIVE DROPS BELOW
Bladder	Resident	-85
Bladder	Visitor	-80
Comfort	Resident	-90
Comfort	Visitor	-60
Energy	Resident	-80
Energy	Visitor	-70
Hunger	Resident	-80
Hunger	Visitor	-40

...ygiene

...d Hygiene will never kill a Sim, although it may ...iously gross out others in the immediate vicinity. ...ving this problem is easy—have your Sims wash ...eir hands or take a shower. You can also ...mbine Hygiene with other Motives. Taking a ...th boosts the Hygiene and Comfort scores, while ...oak in the hot tub (with friends) rewards the ...giene, Comfort, Social, and Fun Motive bars.

Bladder

If you can't satisfy the Bladder urge, you'll be cleaning up puddles on the floor. Just make sure you find a bathroom before the Motive bar turns full red. A Sloppy Sim creates an additional risk by not regularly flushing the toilet. If you don't issue timely reminders, the toilet could get clogged, causing a major mess.

TIP

Pay special attention to the Bladder bar when your Sim spends time at the Beverage Bar or drinks a lot of coffee.

CAUTION

The Hygiene score takes a nose dive if a Sim can't get to the bathroom in time and pees on the floor.

Fig. 2-5. This Sim's Bladder is not quite full, but unless his guest vacates the bathroom soon, he could be in trouble.

Energy

We're talking sleep, pure and simple. Ideally, a good night's sleep should turn the bar completely green. This will happen at varying rates, depending upon the quality of the mattress, so you can get by on less sleep if you splurge for an expensive bed. If your Sim can't get to the bedroom or a couch before the Energy bar turns completely red, the floor becomes your only option. If this happens, wake your Sim and find the closest bed. A night on the hard floor will degrade your Sim's Comfort level to zero, while only restoring partial energy.

If your Sim stays up too late playing computer games, a shot of espresso provides a temporary Energy boost, although it will also fill the Bladder at an increased rate. Espresso has a powerful effect, but it takes longer to consume, which could be a problem if the car pool driver is honking.

Fig. 2-6. It never hurts to send your kids to bed early, because if they are tired in the morning, a coffee jolt is not an option.

Fun

Sims like to cut loose from the daily grind and have Fun, but depending upon their personalities, they prefer different activities. For example, a Playful Sim leans toward computer games, pinball machines, and train sets; while a more Serious Sim would rather sit down to a quiet game of chess or spend a few minutes gazing at a painting.

Fig. 2-7. These two Sims enjoy a game of pool after work.

Kids need to have more Fun than adults, and the effects of a single play session deteriorate faster for kids than for their older counterparts. Hence, it is a good idea to fill the house with plenty of juvenile diversions if you have children.

There are four different types of Fun activities: Extended, One-Time, Timed, and Endless. The following lists and tables provide additional information, including exit factors, for these pursuits.

Extended Fun Activities

Sims exit the following extended activities after reaching the maximum Fun score for their personality types. Hence, a Playful, Active Sim will stay on the basketball court longer than a Serious Sim.

asketball Hoop

ookshelf (reading)

ollhouse

omputer (playing games)

inball Machine

lay Structure

tereo

oy Box

ain Set

V

R Glasses

e-Time Fun Activities

e following activities raise a Sim's Fun score once
h each interaction. It may take several
eractions with the same activity for a Sim to
ch the maximum Fun level.

BJECT	ACTION
quarium	Feed or watch fish
aby	Play
iving Board	Dive into the pool
spresso Machine	Drink espresso
ountain	View
ava Lamp	View
ainting	View
culpture	View

ed (Pre-set) Fun Activities

with the one-time activities listed above, a Sim
y need to repeat the following activities to
ieve maximum Fun points.

hess Set

ool Table

Endless Fun

• **Hot Tub:** A Sim will stay in the tub until Fun, Comfort, Social, and Hygiene numbers reach maximum levels.

• **Swimming Pool:** A Sim will keep doing laps until another Motive takes effect, or until you assign him or her to another activity.

Social

Sims crave other Sims, especially if they are Outgoing. Although they won't die without socializing, it is a good idea to devote a portion of each day to a group activity, even if it is a simple hot tub session with your Sim's mate, or a family meal.

Fig. 2-8. A casual conversation during breakfast raises this Sim's Social score.

The following table summarizes all of the possible Social interactions between adults and children. We take this one step further in the next chapter, "Interacting with Other Sims," where we examine Relationships.

Adult-Child Interactions

ACTION	ADULT TO ADULT	CHILD TO CHILD	ADULT TO CHILD	CHILD TO ADULT
Apologize	X	—	—	—
Attack	X	X	—	—
Brag	X	X	X	X
Call Here	X	X	X	X
Cheer Up	X	X	X	X
Compliment	X	—	—	—
Dance	X	—	—	—
Entertain	X	X	X	X
Flirt	X	—	—	—
Give Back Rub	X	—	—	—
Give Gift	X	X	X	X
Hug	X	X	X	X
Insult	X	X	X	X
Joke	X	X	X	X
Kiss	X	—	—	—
Say Goodbye	X	X	X	—
Scare	X	X	X	X
Slap	X	—	—	—
Tag	—	X	—	—
Talk	X	X	X	X
Tease	X	X	X	X
Tickle	X	X	X	X

Social Outcome Modifiers

You didn't expect a Sim Social encounter to be simple, did you? When one Sim communicates with another, several calculations determine the outcome. Factors include age (adult or child), sex, mood, and personality traits, not to mention the current state of their Relationship. Also, a Sim with strong Social needs (but few friends) may expect more from an encounter with a Sim who has similar needs.

The following table lists the factors that govern the choices that appear on a Social actions menu. For example, two Sims who are strangers are not likely to have the options to kiss or hug. Additionally, the table lists key factors that determine the eventual outcome.

rel = Relationship	age = Adult/Child
out = Outgoing	social = Social Motive Value
play = Playful	vis = Visitor
ff = Friend Flag	budget = Household Budget
ss = Same Sex	nice = Nice
rom = Romance Flag	body = Body

ial Outcome Factors

TERACTION	FACTORS THAT DETERMINE APPEARANCE ON THE MENU	FACTORS THAT DETERMINE OUTCOME
pologize	rel	mood
ttack	age, nice, mood, rel	body
ack Rub	age, nice, mood, rel, out, ss	rel, out, ss
rag	nice, out, social, rel	rel, mood
eer Up	ff, mood (of friend), nice	rel
ompliment	age, nice, out, mood, rel	rel, mood
ance	age, mood, out, rel	rel, out, mood
tertain	social, out, play, mood, rel	play, rel
irt	age, social, ss, out, mood, rel, rom	rel, mood, ss
ft	vis, budget, nice, mood, rel	rel, mood
ug	age, out, mood, rel, ss	rel, out, mood, ss
sult	nice, mood, rel	nice
ke	play, mood, rel	play, mood, rel
ss	ss, mood, rel, age	rel, mood, ss
are	nice, mood, play, rel	play, mood
ap	age, nice, mood, rel	nice, mood
lk	mood, rel, out	topics match
ase	nice, mood, rel	rel, mood
ckle	social, out, play, active, mood, rel	rel, play

Room

This is a combined rating that analyzes the design and contents of the current room, and translates it into a Room score. Of all the Motives, Room is the least important. However, if you love your Sim, you'll want to create the best possible environment. The most important contributing factors to Room score are:

- **Light:** Sims hate dark rooms, so fill your house with sunlight (windows and paned doors), lamps, and wall lights.
- **Room Size:** Don't cramp your Sims into tiny rooms.
- **Corners:** As mentioned in the "Building a House" chapter, Sims love corners.
- **State of Repair:** Any items that are not functioning properly detract from the Room score (see following list).

Fig. 2-9. Who wouldn't love a kitchen like this? It's bright, roomy, nicely furnished, and packed with high-tech appliances.

Negative Impact on Room Score

- **Trash**
- **Floods**
- **Dirty plates**
- **Meals with flies**
- **Full trash cans/compactors**
- **Dead plants**
- **Puddle or ash pile**
- **Dead fish in aquariums**
- **Dirty objects (shower, toilet, tub)**

The following table lists the positive or negative value of every object in *The Sims*.

Room Score

OBJECT	STATE/TYPE	ROOM SCORE
Aquarium	Fish Alive	25
	Dirty	-25
	Dirty and/or Dead	-50
Ash	N/A	-10
Bar	N/A	20
Bed	Unmade (Any Bed)	-10
	Made Mission	30
	Made (Other than Mission)	10
Chair	Parisienne	25
	Empress	10
Clock (Grandfather)	N/A	50
Computer	Broken	-25
Counter	Barcelona	15
Desk	Redmond	15
Dresser	Antique Armoire	20
	Oak Armoire	10
Fire	N/A	-100

JECT	STATE/TYPE	ROOM SCORE
eplace	Library Edition (No Fire)	20
	Library Edition (Fire)	75
	Worcestershire (No Fire)	15
	Worcestershire (Fire)	60
	Bostonian (No Fire)	10
	Bostonian (Fire)	45
	Modesto (No Fire)	5
	Modesto (Fire)	30
amingo	N/A	10
od	N/A	-25
wers (utdoor)	Healthy	20
wers/Plants door)	Dead	-20
	Healthy	10
	Wilted	0
	Dead	-10
od	Snack (Spoiled)	-15
	Fruitcake (Empty Plate)	-5
	BBQ Group Meal (Spoiled)	-20
	BBQ Single Meal (Spoiled)	-15
	Empty Plate	-10
	Pizza Slice (Spoiled)	-10
	Pizza Box (Spoiled)	-25
	Candy (Spoiled)	-5
	Group Meal (Spoiled)	-20
	Meal (Spoiled)	-25
	Quick Meal (Spoiled)	-20
untain	N/A	25
wers (Gift)	Dead	-10
	Alive	20
mp	Not Broken	10
va Lamp	N/A	20
ewspaper	Old Newspapers	-20
ano	N/A	30

OBJECT	STATE/TYPE	ROOM SCORE
Pinball Machine	Broken	-15
Shower	Broken	-15
Sofa (Deiter or Dolce)	N/A	20
Stereo	Strings	25
Table	Mesa	15
	Parisienne	25
Toilet	Clogged	-10
Train Set	Small	25
Trash Can (Inside)	Full	-20
Trash Compactor	Full	-25
Trash Pile	N/A	-20
TV	Soma	20
	Broken (Any TV)	-15

Object Advertising Values

Earlier in the chapter we mentioned that Sims receive Motive rewards when they select an activity. If you are in complete control of your Sims (Free Will is off), you determine their choices. However, with Free Will on, Sims constantly poll their surroundings to compare which objects are "advertising" the most attractive rewards. The following table includes a Motive profile of every object in *The Sims*.

Object Advertising Values

OBJECT TYPE	POSSIBLE INTERACTIONS	OBJECT VARIATIONS	ADVERTISED MOTIVE	ADVERTISED VALUE	PERSONALITY TRAIT MODIFIER	REDUCED EFFECT (OVER DISTANCE)
Aquarium	Clean & Restock	N/A	Room	30	Neat	Medium
	Feed Fish	N/A	Room	10	Nice	High
		N/A	Fun	10	Playful	High
	Watch Fish	N/A	Fun	10	Playful	High
Ash	Sweep Up	N/A	Energy	23	N/A	Medium
		N/A	Room	50	Neat	Medium
Baby	Play	N/A	Fun	50	Playful	Medium
Bar	Have Drink	N/A	Room	30	N/A	Low
	Grill	Barbecue	Energy	-10	N/A	Low
			Hunger	40	Cooking	Low
Basketball Hoop	Join	N/A	Fun	30	Active	High
		N/A	Social	20	N/A	Medium
		N/A	Energy	-20	N/A	Medium
	Play	N/A	Fun	30	Active	High
		N/A	Energy	-20	N/A	High
Bed	Make Bed	All Beds	Room	25	Neat	High
	Sleep	Double Bed (Cheap Eazzzzze)	Energy	65	N/A	None
		Double Bed (Napoleon)	Energy	67	N/A	None
		Double Bed (Mission)	Energy	70	N/A	None
		Single Bed (Spartan)	Energy	60	N/A	None
		Single Bed (Tyke Nyte)	Energy	63	N/A	None
	Tuck in Kid	All Beds	Energy	160	Nice	None

OBJECT TYPE	POSSIBLE INTERACTIONS	OBJECT VARIATIONS	ADVERTISED MOTIVE	ADVERTISED VALUE	PERSONALITY TRAIT MODIFIER	REDUCED EFFECTS (OVER DISTANCE)
...okcase	Read a Book	Bookcase (Pine)	Fun	10	Serious	High
		Bookcase (Amishim)	Fun	20	Serious	High
		Bookcase (Libri di Regina)	Fun	30	Serious	High
...air (...ving Room)	Sit	Wicker	Comfort	20	N/A	Medium
		Country Class	Comfort	20	N/A	Medium
		Citronel	Comfort	20	N/A	Medium
		Sarrbach	Comfort	20	N/A	Medium
...air (...ining Room)	Sit	Werkbunnst	Comfort	25	N/A	Medium
		Teak	Comfort	25	N/A	Medium
		Empress	Comfort	25	N/A	Medium
		Parisienne	Comfort	25	N/A	Medium
...air (...ffice/Deck)	Sit	Office Chair	Comfort	20	N/A	Medium
		Deck Chair	Comfort	20	N/A	Medium
...air (Recliner)	Nap	Both Recliners	Energy	15	Lazy	High
		Both Recliners	Comfort	20	Lazy	Medium
	Sit	Both Recliners	Comfort	30	Lazy	Medium
...ess	Join	Chess Set	Fun	40	Outgoing	High
			Social	40	N/A	Medium
	Play		Fun	35	Serious	High
...ck (...randfather)	Wind	N/A	Room	40	Neat	High
...ffee (...presso ...achine)	Drink Espresso	N/A	Energy	115	N/A	Medium
		N/A	Fun	10	N/A	High
		N/A	Bladder	-10	N/A	High
...ffeemaker	Drink Coffee	N/A	Bladder	-5	N/A	High
		N/A	Energy	115	N/A	Medium

OBJECT TYPE	POSSIBLE INTERACTIONS	OBJECT VARIATIONS	ADVERTISED MOTIVE	ADVERTISED VALUE	PERSONALITY TRAIT MODIFIER	REDUCED EFFECT (OVER DISTANCE)
Computer	Play	Moneywell	Fun	30	Playful	High
		Microscotch	Fun	35	Playful	High
		Brahma	Fun	40	Playful	High
		Marco	Fun	50	Playful	High
	Turn Off	All Computers	Energy	220	Neat	Medium
Dollhouse	Play	N/A	Fun	30	Playful	High
	Watch	N/A	Fun	30	Playful	Medium
		N/A	Social	30	N/A	Medium
Easel	Paint	N/A	Fun	20	N/A	High
Flamingo	Kick	N/A	Mood	15	Grouchy	High
	View	N/A	Fun	10	Playful	High
Flood	Clean	N/A	Room	80	Neat	High
Flowers (Outdoor)	Stomp On	N/A	Mood	10	Grouchy	High
	Water	N/A	Room	20	Neat	Medium
Flowers/Plants (Indoor)	Throw Out	N/A	Room	50	Neat	Medium
	Water	N/A	Room	25	Neat	Medium
Food	Clean	All Meal/ Snack Types	Room	20	Neat	Medium
	Prepare and Eat	BBQ Group Meal	Hunger	90	N/A	Low
		BBQ Single	Hunger	80	N/A	Low
		Candy	Hunger	30	N/A	Low
		Fruitcake (Group Meal)	Hunger	30	N/A	Low
		Fruitcake (Slice)	Hunger	80	N/A	Low
		Light Meal	Hunger	80	N/A	Low
		Pizza Box	Hunger	90	N/A	Low
		Pizza Slice	Hunger	80	N/A	Low
		Regular Group Meal	Hunger	90	N/A	Low
		Regular Single Meal	Hunger	80	N/A	Low
		Snack	Hunger	25	N/A	Low

OBJECT TYPE	POSSIBLE INTERACTIONS	OBJECT VARIATIONS	ADVERTISED MOTIVE	ADVERTISED VALUE	PERSONALITY TRAIT MODIFIER	REDUCED EFFECTS (OVER DISTANCE)
ountain	Play	N/A	Fun	10	Shy	High
efrigerator	Have Meal	All Fridges	Hunger	65	N/A	Low
	Have Snack	Llamark	Hunger	20	N/A	Low
		Porcina	Hunger	30	N/A	Low
		Freeze Secret	Hunger	40	N/A	Low
	Have Quick Meal	All Fridges	Hunger	55	N/A	Low
	Serve Meal	All Fridges	Hunger	70	Cooking	Low
		All Fridges	Energy	-10	N/A	Low
ift (Flowers)	Clean	N/A	Room	30	Neat	Medium
ot Tub	Get In	N/A	Fun	45	Lazy	High
		N/A	Comfort	50	N/A	High
		N/A	Social	25	Outgoing	Medium
		N/A	Hygiene	5	N/A	Medium
	Join	N/A	Comfort	30	N/A	Low
		N/A	Fun	50	Outgoing	Low
		N/A	Social	50	N/A	Low
		N/A	Hygiene	5	N/A	Medium
va Lamp	Turn On	N/A	Room	5	N/A	High
		N/A	Fun	5	N/A	High
ailbox	Get Mail	N/A	Comfort	10	N/A	High
		N/A	Hunger	10	N/A	High
		N/A	Hygiene	10	N/A	High
		N/A	Room	10	N/A	High
edicine abinet	Brush Teeth	N/A	Hygiene	25	Neat	Medium
ewspaper	Clean Up	N/A	Room	50	Neat	Medium
	Read	N/A	Fun	5	Serious	High
ainting	View	N/A	Fun	5	Serious	High
one	Answer	N/A	Fun	50	N/A	Medium
		N/A	Comfort	50	N/A	Medium
		N/A	Social	50	N/A	Medium
ano	Play	N/A	Fun	40	Strong Creativity	High
	Watch	N/A	Fun	70	N/A	Medium
		N/A	Social	10	N/A	Medium

OBJECT TYPE	POSSIBLE INTERACTIONS	OBJECT VARIATIONS	ADVERTISED MOTIVE	ADVERTISED VALUE	PERSONALITY TRAIT MODIFIER	REDUCED EFFECT (OVER DISTANCE)
Pinball Machine	Join	N/A	Fun	50	N/A	Medium
		N/A	Social	30	N/A	Medium
	Play	N/A	Fun	40	Playful	High
Play Structure	Join	N/A	Fun	60	Playful	Medium
		N/A	Social	40	N/A	Medium
	Play	N/A	Fun	60	Playful	Medium
Pool Diving Board	Dive In	N/A	Fun	35	Active	High
		N/A	Energy	-10	N/A	High
Pool Table	Join	N/A	Fun	50	Playful	Low
		N/A	Social	40	N/A	Low
	Play	N/A	Fun	45	Playful	High
Sculpture	View	Scylla and Charybdis	Fun	6	Serious	High
		Bust of Athena	Fun	5	Serious	High
		Large Black Slab	Fun	8	Serious	High
		China Vase	Fun	7	Serious	High
Shower	Clean	N/A	Room	20	Neat	High
	Take a Shower	N/A	Hygiene	50	Neat	Medium
Sink	Wash Hands	N/A	Hygiene	10	Neat	High
Sofa/Loveseat	Nap	All Sofas/ Loveseats	Energy	40	Lazy	High
		All Sofas/ Loveseats	Comfort	5	Lazy	High
	Sit	All Sofas/ Loveseats	Comfort	30	Lazy	Medium
		Garden Bench	Comfort	30	Lazy	Medium
Stereo	Dance	Boom Box	Social	40	Outgoing	High
			Fun	50	Active	High
		Zimantz Hi-Fi	Social	50	Outgoing	High
			Fun	60	Active	High
		Strings Theory	Social	60	Outgoing	High
			Fun	70	Active	High
	Join	Boom Box	Social	40	Outgoing	Low

OBJECT TYPE	POSSIBLE INTERACTIONS	OBJECT VARIATIONS	ADVERTISED MOTIVE	ADVERTISED VALUE	PERSONALITY TRAIT MODIFIER	REDUCED EFFECTS (OVER DISTANCE)
...ereo			Fun	40	Outgoing	Low
		Zimantz Hi-Fi	Social	50	Outgoing	Low
			Fun	40	Outgoing	Low
		Strings Theory	Social	60	Outgoing	Low
			Fun	40	Outgoing	Low
	Turn Off	All Stereos	Energy	220	Neat	Medium
	Turn On	Boom Box	Fun	25	Playful	High
		Zimantz Hi-Fi	Fun	25	Playful	High
		Strings Theory	Fun	30	Playful	High
...ilet	Clean	Both Toilets	Room	40	Neat	High
	Flush	Hygeia-O-Matic	Room	30	Neat	High
	Unclog	Both Toilets	Room	50	Neat	High
	Use	Hygeia-O-Matic	Bladder	50	N/A	Low
		Flush Force	Bladder	70	N/A	Low
...mbstone/ ...n	Mourn (first 24 hours)	N/A	Bladder	5	N/A	Low
		N/A	Comfort	50	N/A	Low
		N/A	Energy	5	N/A	Low
		N/A	Fun	50	N/A	Low
		N/A	Hunger	5	N/A	Low
		N/A	Hygiene	50	N/A	Low
		N/A	Social	50	N/A	Low
		N/A	Room	50	N/A	Low
	Mourn (second 48 hours)	N/A	Bladder	0	N/A	Low
		N/A	Comfort	30	N/A	Low
		N/A	Energy	0	N/A	Low
		N/A	Fun	30	N/A	Low
		N/A	Hunger	0	N/A	Low
		N/A	Hygiene	30	N/A	Low
		N/A	Social	30	N/A	Low
		N/A	Room	30	N/A	Low
...y Box	Play	N/A	Fun	55	Playful	Medium

OBJECT TYPE	POSSIBLE INTERACTIONS	OBJECT VARIATIONS	ADVERTISED MOTIVE	ADVERTISED VALUE	PERSONALITY TRAIT MODIFIER	REDUCED EFFECT (OVER DISTANCE)
Train Set (Large)	Play	N/A	Fun	40	N/A	Medium
	Watch	N/A	Fun	40	N/A	Low
		N/A	Social	40	N/A	Low
Train Set (Small)	Play	N/A	Fun	45	Playful	Medium
	Watch	N/A	Fun	20	N/A	Medium
		N/A	Social	30	N/A	Medium
Trash Can (Inside)	Empty Trash	N/A	Room	30	Neat	Medium
Trash Compactor	Empty Trash	N/A	Room	30	N/A	High
Trash Pile	Clean	N/A	Room	75	Neat	Medium
Bathtub	Clean	All Tubs	Room	20	Neat	High
	Bathe	Justa	Hygiene	50	Neat	Medium
		Justa	Comfort	20	N/A	Medium
		Sani-Queen	Hygiene	60	Neat	Medium
		Sani-Queen	Comfort	25	N/A	Medium
		Hydrothera	Hygiene	70	Neat	Medium
		Hydrothera	Comfort	30	N/A	Medium
TV	Join	Monochrome	Fun	20	Lazy	High
		Trottco	Fun	30	Lazy	High
		Soma Plasma	Fun	45	Lazy	High
	Turn Off	All TVs	Energy	220	Neat	Medium
	Turn On	Monochrome	Fun	18	Lazy	High
		Trottco	Fun	35	Lazy	High
		Soma Plasma	Fun	49	Lazy	High
	Watch TV	Monochrome	Fun	18	Lazy	High
		Trottco	Fun	28	Lazy	High
		Soma Plasma	Fun	42	Lazy	High
VR Glasses	Play	N/A	Fun	60	Playful	High

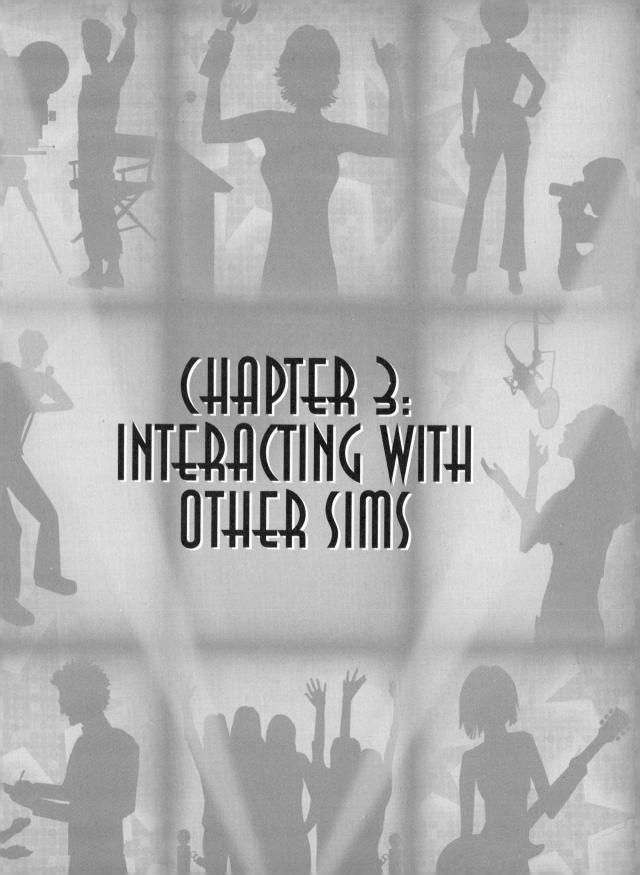

CHAPTER 3: INTERACTING WITH OTHER SIMS

Introduction

Once you get beyond the dark attraction of watching jilted Sims slap their rivals, or obnoxious Sims insulting their friends, you realize that Relationships are very important to your Sims' quality of life, and even to the advancement of their careers. In this chapter, we introduce you to the world of Relationships, covering the possible events that occur when two Sims come together verbally or physically. Our goal here is to lay down the ground rules. We'll offer hands-on tips for building and maintaining Relationships in the "All in the Family" chapter.

Relationship Scores

Icons representing a Sim's friendships, or lack thereof, appear in the screen's lower-right corner when you click on the Relationships icon (just above the Job icon). The scoring system ranges from below 0 (not good) to 100, which is reserved for one or more significant others. A relationship is considered a true friendship if the score climbs above 50. Only these Relationships are considered when the game calculates career advancements. Consult the next chapter, "9 to 5—Climbing the Career Ladder," for more information on promotion requirements.

Fig. 3-1. This Sim Dad is clicking on all cylinders with his wife, but he needs to spend more time with the kids.

Social Interactions

All Sim Relationships develop from Social interactions. If you don't spend quality time wit your friends, the Relationships will deteriorate their own, at a rate of two points per day. Of course, if you interact poorly, the rate accelerate dramatically. In the following sections, we revie the myriad communication choices that are available during the game (grouped alphabetica by the active action). At any given time, your choice will vary, depending upon the level of yc friendship, and whether or not your Sim is actin like a jerk!

Good Old Conversation

The easiest way to cultivate a new friendship is talk. Sims communicate with each other using S Speak, a delightful chatter that you actually be to understand (yes, we have played this game v too much!). Adults and kids have favorite topic within their peer groups. These topics are randomly assigned by the game during the Sim creation process. Additionally, kids and adults h special cross-generational topics that are only u with each other. Active topics are displayed in thought balloons during the game, as shown in figure 3-2.

Fig. 3-2. Pets a good common ground for cor sation betwee adults and kid

When a conversation is going well, you see a
n plus sign over one or both of the Sims.
versely, when talk deteriorates into the
er, you'll see red minus signs. The following
es list positive and negative communications,
ding each potential outcome and the
esponding effect on Social and Relationship
es. For our purposes, an outcome is positive if
oduces an increase in one or both scores.
n scores drop or stay the same, it is
idered a negative outcome.

Fig. 3-3. When two or more people enter a hot tub, the conversations begin spontaneously.

tive Communications

ERACTION	RESPONSE	RELATIONSHIP CHANGE	SOCIAL SCORE CHANGE
ologize	Accept	10	15
Apologized To	Accept	10	15
ag	Good	5	13
Bragged To	Good	5	7
eer Up	Good	5	7
eer Up	Neutral	0	5
Cheered Up	Good	10	10
Cheered Up	Neutral	0	5
mpliment	Accept	5	5
Complimented	Accept	5	11
tertain	Laugh	4	7
Entertained	Laugh	8	13
rt	Good	5	13
Flirted With	Good	10	13
ke	Laugh	5	13
ke	Giggle	2	7
ten to Joke	Laugh	7	13
ten to Joke	Giggle	3	7
are	Laugh	5	10
lkHigh Interest	Topic	3	5
lkLike	Topic	3	5
oup Talk	N/A	1	8
ase	Giggle	5	7

Negative Communications

INTERACTION	RESPONSE	RELATIONSHIP CHANGE	SOCIAL SCORE CHANGE
Apologize	Reject	-10	0
Be Apologized To	Reject	-10	0
Brag	Bad	-5	0
Be Bragged To	Bad	-5	0
Cheer Up	Bad	-3	0
Be Cheered Up	Bad	-10	0
Compliment	Reject	-10	0
Be Complimented	Reject	-7	0
Entertain	Boo	-15	0
Be Entertained	Boo	-7	0
Flirt	Refuse	-10	-17
Flirt	Ignore	-5	0
Be Flirted With	Refuse	-10	0
Be Flirted With	Ignore	0	0
Insult	Cry	5	0
Insult	Stoic	0	3
Insult	Angry	-10	7
Be Insulted	Cry	-12	-13
Be Insulted	Stoic	-5	-5
Be Insulted	Angry	-14	-7
Joke	Uninterested	-6	0
Listen to Joke	Uninterested	-7	0
Scare	Angry	-5	0
Be Scared	Angry	-10	0
TalkDislike	Topic	-3	3
TalkHate	Topic	-3	3
Tease	Cry	-4	0
Be Teased	Cry	-13	-7

ysical Contact

en a Relationship moves past the 50-point threshold, you begin to see new options on the Social
raction menu. Instead of just talking, you find new items including Hug, Give Back Rub, Flirt,
Kiss. It all depends upon how your Relationship is progressing and what the other Sim is looking
n the current interaction. The following tables include information on positive and negative
ical events.

tive Physical Events

ERACTION	RESPONSE	RELATIONSHIP CHANGE	SOCIAL SCORE CHANGE
ve Back Rub	Good	5	7
ceive Back Rub	Good	9	13
nce	Accept	8	13
Danced With	Accept	10	13
ve Gift	Accept	5	7
ceive Gift	Accept	10	13
g	Good	7	15
g	Tentative	2	7
Hugged	Good	8	15
Hugged	Tentative	4	7
ss	Passion	12	20
ss	Polite	5	10
Kissed	Passion	12	20
Kissed	Polite	5	10
kle	Accept	5	13
Tickled	Accept	8	13

Negative Physical Events

INTERACTION	RESPONSE	RELATIONSHIP CHANGE	SOCIAL SCORE CHANGE
Attack	Win Fight	-5	10
Attack	Lose Fight	-10	-20
Give Back Rub	Bad	-7	0
Receive Back Rub	Bad	-10	0
Dance	Refuse	-5	0
Be Danced With	Refuse	-5	0
Give Gift	Stomp	-15	0
Receive Gift	Stomp	-5	0
Hug	Refuse	-10	0
Be Hugged	Refuse	-10	0
Kiss	Deny	-15	5
Be Kissed	Deny	-10	0
Slap	Cry	0	3
Slap	Slap Back	-10	-7
Be Slapped	Cry	-20	-17
Be Slapped	Slap Back	-15	7
Tickle	Refuse	-5	0
Be Tickled	Refuse	-8	0

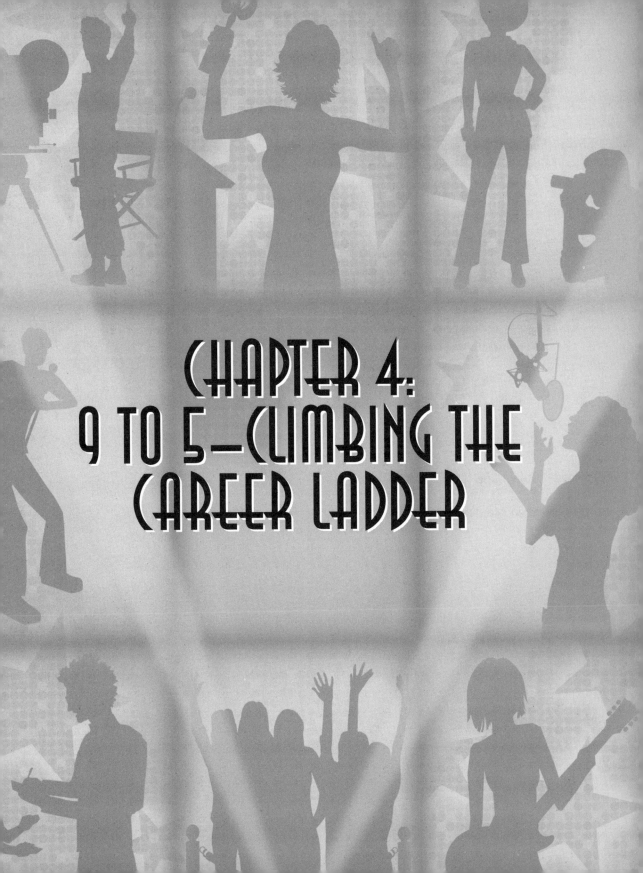

CHAPTER 4:
9 TO 5—CLIMBING THE CAREER LADDER

Introduction

When you first start playing *The Sims*, it's easy to get lost in the element. There's so much to explore and experience, and with more than enough money to furnish your house and buy a few toys, you can just hang out and live the good Sim-life. But, reality sets in sooner than you would like, and you must find a job. In this chapter we show you how to select a career, nurture the Skills necessary to earn the first few promotions, and finally, stockpile enough friends (it's called networking) to make the big bucks and zoom to the top of your field. For easy reference, we include comprehensive career tables that contain everything you need to know about the 10 Sim careers, including advancement requirements for all 10 pay levels.

Your First Job

Every Sim house receives a daily copy of the *Sim City Times* that includes a single job posting. You can take the first job you see, or buy a computer and view three jobs a day. There is no rush—you have enough money to get by for several days.

Fig. 4-1. Today's job posting is for a test driver.

TIP

You can enjoy the free use of a computer by buying it, checking the want ads, and then returning it the same day for a full refund. Keep this up until you find the job you want. Then, later when you have more disposable cash, you can buy—and keep—a computer.

A Military job is usually available on the computer. This is an excellent first career, with a starting salary of §250. Furthermore, it remains highest paying of the 10 careers through the fir three advances. A Law Enforcement position is a close second.

Fig. 4-2. This tw commando fam takes home §32 each as membe of the Elite Forc (Level 2—Milita Career).

If you would rather take your time and sort through all 10 job tracks, the following table wi help you choose a career that is suited to your Sim's personality traits.

...eer Choices

...REER TRACK	NECESSARY SKILLS	RELATED PERSONALITY TRAITS
...siness	Logic, Charisma	Outgoing
...tertainment	Charisma, Creativity	Outgoing, Playful
...w Enforcement	Logic, Body	Active
...fe of Crime	Creativity, Charisma	Playful, Outgoing
...edicine	Logic, Body	Active
...ilitary	Repair, Body	Active
...litics	Charisma, Logic	Outgoing
...o Athlete	Body, Charisma	Active, Outgoing
...ience	Logic, Creativity	Playful
...reme	Creativity, Body/Charisma (tie)	Playful, Active, Outgoing

...veloping Your Skills

...er you decide on a career, focus on developing the appropriate Skills needed for advancement. It is ...ortant to remember that Sims do not study on their own. You need to direct your Sim to one of the ...vities listed in the Skill Enhancement table on the following page.

TIP

...n the control panel, click on the Job icon to ...splay your Sim's current Skill bars (see figure 4-... A white line designates the minimum level of ...ill needed for the next promotion. Other ...ctors contribute to earning a promotion, but ...ithout the Skill requirement, you have ...solutely no chance for advancement to the ...xt level.

Fig. 4-3. This Sim needs to boost his Body Skill one more notch, so he is scheduled for a session on the exercise machine right after lunch.

Skill Enhancement

SKILL	METHOD OF ENHANCEMENT	NOTES
Cooking	Bookshelf (Study Cooking)	Any type of bookshelf will suffice.
Mechanical	Bookshelf (Study Mechanical)	Any type of bookshelf will suffice.
Body	Exercise Machine (Work Out)	Exercise machine increases Skill four times faster than the pool. Active Sims improve their Skill at a higher rate.
	Pool (Swim)	See above.
Charisma	Mirrors or Medicine Cabinet (Practice Speech)	Outgoing Sims acquire Skill more quickly
	Easel (Paint)	Playful Sims acquire Skill more quickly.
	Piano (Play)	Playful Sims acquire Skill more quickly.
Logic	Chessboard (Play)	Playing with another Sim generates Social points.

Fig. 4-4. A session on the exercise bench nets a Body point for this Sim.

Sim Career Tracks

The following tables include the salaries, hours, pool vehicles, and job level requirements for each level of the 10 Sim career tracks. The Daily Motive Decay value shows which Motives deteriorate while the Sim is on the job.

Requirements for Level 1 Positions

POSITION	PAY	HOURS	CAR POOL VEHICLE	COOKING	REPAIR	CHARISMA	BODY	LOGIC	CREATIVITY	FAMILY/ FRIENDS	DAILY MOTIVE DECAY						
											HUNGER	COMFORT	HYGIENE	BLADDER	ENERGY	FUN	SOCIAL
Mail Room	§120	9 a.m.–3 p.m	Junker	0	0	0	0	0	0	0	0	0	0	0	-30	0	0
Waiter Waitress	§100	9 a.m.–3 p.m.	Junker	0	0	0	0	0	0	0	0	0	0	0	-30	0	0
Security Guard	§240	12 a.m.–6 a.m.	Squad Car	0	0	0	0	0	0	0	0	0	0	0	-30	0	0
Pickpocket	§140	9 a.m.–3 p.m.	Junker	0	0	0	0	0	0	0	0	0	0	0	-30	0	0
Medical Technician	§200	9 a.m.–3 p.m.	Junker	0	0	0	0	0	0	0	0	0	0	0	-30	0	0
Recruit	§250	6 a.m.–12 p.m.	Military Jeep	0	0	0	0	0	0	0	0	0	-15	0	-30	0	0
Campaign Work	§220	9 a.m.–6 p.m.	Junker	0	0	0	0	0	0	0	0	0	0	0	-30	0	0
Team Mascot	§110	12 p.m.–6 p.m.	Junker	0	0	0	0	0	0	0	0	0	-5	0	-35	0	0
Test Subject	§155	9 a.m.–3 p.m.	Junker	0	0	0	0	0	0	0	0	0	0	0	-30	0	0
Daredevil	§175	9 a.m.–3 p.m.	Junker	0	0	0	0	0	0	0	0	0	0	0	-30	0	0

Requirements for Level 2 Positions

POSITION	PAY	HOURS	CAR POOL VEHICLE	COOKING	REPAIR	CHARISMA	BODY	LOGIC	CREATIVITY	FAMILY/ FRIENDS	DAILY MOTIVE DECAY						
											HUNGER	COMFORT	HYGIENE	BLADDER	ENERGY	FUN	SOCIAL
Executive Assistant	§180	9 a.m.–4 p.m	Junker	0	0	0	0	0	0	0	0	0	0	0	-34	-2	0
Extra	§150	9 a.m.–3 p.m.	Junker	0	0	0	0	0	0	0	0	0	0	0	-34	-2	0
Cadet	§320	9 a.m.–3 p.m.	Squad Car	0	0	0	0	0	0	0	0	0	0	0	-34	-2	0
Bagman	§200	11 p.m.–7 a.m.	Junker	0	0	0	0	0	0	0	0	0	0	0	-34	-2	0
Paramedic	§275	11 p.m.–5 a.m.	Junker	0	0	0	0	0	0	0	0	0	0	0	-34	-2	0
Elite Forces	§325	7 a.m.–1 p.m.	Military Jeep	0	0	0	0	0	0	0	0	0	-15	0	-34	-2	0
Intern	§300	9 a.m.–3 p.m.	Junker	0	0	0	0	0	0	0	0	0	0	0	-34	-2	0
Minor Leaguer	§170	9 a.m.–3 p.m.	Junker	0	0	0	0	0	0	0	0	0	-10	0	-40	-2	0
Lab Assistant	§230	11 p.m.–5 a.m.	Junker	0	0	0	0	0	0	0	0	0	0	0	-34	-2	0
Bungee Jump Instructor	§250	9 a.m.–3 p.m.	Junker	0	0	0	0	0	0	0	0	0	0	0	-34	-2	0

Requirements for Level 3 Positions

CAREER TRACK	POSITION	PAY	HOURS	CAR POOL VEHICLE	COOKING	REPAIR	CHARISMA	BODY	LOGIC	CREATIVITY	FAMILY/ FRIENDS	DAILY MOTIVE DECAY					
												HUNGER	COMFORT	HYGIENE	BLADDER	ENERGY	FUN
Business	Field Sales Rep	§250	9 a.m.–4 p.m.	Junker	0	2	0	0	0	0	0	-3	0	-5	0	-38	-4
Entertainment	Bit Player	§200	9 a.m.–3 p.m.	Junker	0	0	2	0	0	0	0	-3	0	-5	0	-38	-4
Law Enforcement	Patrol Officer	§380	5 p.m.–1 a.m.	Squad Car	0	0	0	2	0	0	0	-3	0	-5	0	-38	-4
Life of Crime	Bookie	§275	12 p.m.–7 p.m.	Standard Car	0	0	0	2	0	0	0	-3	0	-5	0	-38	-4
Medicine	Nurse	§340	9 a.m.–3 p.m.	Standard Car	0	2	0	0	0	0	0	-3	0	-5	0	-38	-4
Military	Drill Instructor	§250	8 a.m.–2 p.m.	Military Jeep	0	0	0	2	0	0	0	-3	0	-20	0	-38	-4
Politics	Lobbyist	§360	9 a.m.–3 p.m.	Standard Car	0	0	2	0	0	0	0	-3	0	-5	0	-38	-4
Pro Athlete	Rookie	§230	9 a.m.–3 p.m.	Junker	0	0	0	2	0	0	0	-3	0	-15	0	-45	-2
Science	Field Researcher	§320	9 a.m.–3 p.m.	Standard Car	0	0	0	0	2	0	0	-3	0	-5	0	-38	-4
Xtreme	Whitewater Guide	§325	9 a.m.–3 p.m.	SUV	0	0	0	2	0	0	1	-3	0	-10	0	-45	-4

Requirements for Level 4 Positions

CAREER TRACK	POSITION	PAY	HOURS	CAR POOL VEHICLE	COOKING	REPAIR	CHARISMA	BODY	LOGIC	CREATIVITY	FAMILY/ FRIENDS	DAILY MOTIVE DECAY					
												HUNGER	COMFORT	HYGIENE	BLADDER	ENERGY	FUN
Business	Junior Executive	§320	9 a.m.–4 p.m.	Standard Car	0	2	2	0	0	0	1	-7	0	-10	0	-42	-7
Entertainment	Stunt Double	§275	9 a.m.–4 p.m.	Standard Car	0	0	2	2	0	0	2	-7	0	-10	0	-42	-7
Law Enforcement	Desk Sergeant	§440	9 a.m.–3 p.m.	Squad Car	0	2	0	2	0	0	1	-7	0	-10	0	-42	-7
Life of Crime	Con Artist	§350	9 a.m.–3 p.m.	Standard Car	0	0	1	2	0	1	2	-7	0	-10	0	-42	-7
Medicine	Intern	§410	9 a.m.–6 p.m.	Standard Car	0	2	0	2	0	0	2	-7	0	-10	0	-42	-7
Military	Junior Officer	§450	9 a.m.–3 p.m.	Military Jeep	0	1	2	2	0	0	0	-7	0	-20	0	-42	-8
Politics	Campaign Manager	§430	9 a.m.–6 p.m.	Standard Car	0	0	2	0	1	0	2	-7	0	-10	0	-42	-7
Pro Athlete	Starter	§300	9 a.m.–3 p.m.	Standard Car	0	0	0	5	0	0	1	-7	0	-20	0	-50	-2
Science	Science Teacher	§375	9 a.m.–4 p.m.	Standard Car	0	0	1	0	3	0	1	-7	0	-10	0	-40	-7
Xtreme	Xtreme Circuit Pro	§400	9 a.m.–3 p.m.	SUV	0	1	0	4	0	0	2	-7	0	-20	0	-50	-2

quirements for Level 5 Positions

R	POSITION	PAY	HOURS	CAR POOL VEHICLE	COOKING	REPAIR	CHARISMA	BODY	LOGIC	CREATIVITY	FAMILY/FRIENDS	DAILY MOTIVE DECAY						
												HUNGER	COMFORT	HYGIENE	BLADDER	ENERGY	FUN	SOCIAL
ss	Executive	§400	9 a.m.–4 p.m.	Standard Car	0	2	2	0	2	0	3	-10	0	-15	0	-46	-10	0
inment	B-Movie Star	§375	10 a.m.–5 p.m.	Standard Car	0	0	3	3	0	1	4	-10	0	-15	0	-46	-10	0
	Vice Squad	§490	10 p.m.–4 a.m.	Squad	0	3	0	4	0	0	2	-10	0	-15	0	-46	-10	0
Crime	Getaway Driver	§425	5 p.m.–1 a.m.	Standard Car	0	2	1	2	0	2	3	-10	0	-10	0	-46	-10	0
ne	Resident	§480	9 p.m.–4 a.m.	Standard Car	0	3	0	2	2	0	3	-10	0	-15	0	-46	-10	0
y	Counter-Intelligence	§500	9 a.m.–3 p.m.	Military Jeep	1	1	2	4	0	0	0	-10	0	-25	0	-46	-12	0
	City Council Member	§485	9 a.m.–3 p.m.	Town Car	0	0	3	1	1	0	4	-10	0	-15	0	-46	-8	0
hlete	All-Star	§385	9 a.m.–3 p.m.	SUV	0	1	1	6	0	0	3	-10	0	-25	0	-55	-3	0
e	Project Leader	§450	9 a.m.–5 p.m.	Standard Car	0	0	2	0	4	1	3	-10	0	-12	0	-43	-8	0
e	Bush Pilot	§475	9 a.m.–3 p.m.	SUV	1	2	0	4	1	0	3	-10	0	-15	0	-46	-5	-10

quirements for Level 6 Positions

R	POSITION	PAY	HOURS	CAR POOL VEHICLE	COOKING	REPAIR	CHARISMA	BODY	LOGIC	CREATIVITY	FAMILY/FRIENDS	DAILY MOTIVE DECAY						
												HUNGER	COMFORT	HYGIENE	BLADDER	ENERGY	FUN	SOCIAL
ss	Senior Manager	§520	9 a.m.–4 p.m.	Standard Car	0	2	3	0	3	2	6	-14	0	-20	0	-50	-13	0
ainment	Supporting Player	§500	10 a.m.–6 p.m.	Limo	0	1	4	4	0	2	6	-14	0	-20	0	-50	-13	0
ement	Detective	§540	9 a.m.–3 p.m.	Squad Car	1	3	1	5	1	0	4	-14	0	-20	0	-50	-13	0
Crime	Bank Robber	§530	3 p.m.–11 p.m.	Town Car	0	3	2	3	1	2	4	-14	0	-15	0	-50	-13	-5
ne	GP	§550	10 a.m.–6 p.m.	Town Car	0	3	1	3	4	0	4	-14	0	-20	0	-50	-13	0
y	Flight Officer	§550	9 a.m.–3 p.m.	Military Jeep	1	2	4	4	1	0	1	-14	0	-28	0	-50	-15	0
s	State Assembly-person	§540	9 a.m.–4 p.m.	Town Car	0	0	4	2	1	1	6	-14	0	-20	0	-50	-12	-3
hlete	MVP	§510	9 a.m.–3 p.m.	SUV	0	2	2	7	0	0	5	-14	0	-30	0	-60	-4	0
e	Inventor	§540	10 a.m.–7 p.m.	Town Car	0	2	2	0	4	3	4	-14	0	-15	0	-45	-9	-8
e	Mountain Climber	§550	9 a.m.–3 p.m.	SUV	1	4	0	6	1	0	4	-14	0	-30	0	-60	0	0

Requirements for Level 7 Positions

CAREER TRACK	POSITION	PAY	HOURS	CAR POOL VEHICLE	COOKING	REPAIR	CHARISMA	BODY	LOGIC	CREATIVITY	FAMILY/ FRIENDS	DAILY MOTIVE DECAY						
												HUNGER	COMFORT	HYGIENE	BLADDER	ENERGY	FUN	SO
Business	Vice President	§660	9 a.m. –5 p.m.	Town Car	0	2	4	2	4	2	8	-18	0	-25	0	-54	-16	
Entertainment	TV Star	§650	10 a.m. –6 p.m.	Limo	0	1	6	5	0	3	8	-18	0	-25	0	-54	-16	
Law Enforcement	Lieutenant	§590	9 a.m. –3 p.m.	Limo	1	3	2	5	3	1	6	-18	0	-25	0	-54	-16	
Life of Crime	Cat Burglar	§640	9 p.m. –3 a.m.	Town Car	1	3	2	5	2	3	6	-18	0	-20	0	-54	-16	
Medicine	Specialist	§625	10 p.m. –4 a.m.	Town Car	0	4	2	4	4	1	5	-18	0	-25	0	-54	-16	
Military	Senior Officer	§580	9 a.m. –3 p.m.	Military Jeep	1	3	4	5	3	0	3	-18	0	-31	0	-55	-20	
Politics	Congress-person	§600	9 a.m. –3 p.m.	Town Car	0	0	4	3	3	2	9	-18	0	-25	0	-54	-18	
Pro Athlete	Superstar	§680	9 a.m. –4 p.m.	SUV	1	2	3	8	0	0	7	-18	0	-35	0	-65	-5	
Science	Scholar	§640	10 a.m. –3 p.m.	Town Car	0	4	2	0	6	4	5	-18	0	-20	0	-48	-10	-
Xtreme	Photo-journalist	§650	9 a.m. –3 p.m.	SUV	1	5	2	6	1	3	5	-18	0	-25	0	-54	-16	

Requirements for Level 8 Positions

CAREER TRACK	POSITION	PAY	HOURS	CAR POOL VEHICLE	COOKING	REPAIR	CHARISMA	BODY	LOGIC	CREATIVITY	FAMILY/ FRIENDS	DAILY MOTIVE DECAY						
												HUNGER	COMFORT	HYGIENE	BLADDER	ENERGY	FUN	SO
Business	President	§800	9 a.m. –5 p.m.	Town Car	0	2	5	2	6	3	10	-22	0	-30	0	-58	-19	
Entertainment	Feature Star	§900	5 p.m. –1 a.m.	Limo	0	2	7	6	0	4	10	-22	0	-30	0	-58	-19	
Law Enforcement	SWAT Team Leader	§625	9 a.m. –3 p.m.	Limo	1	4	3	6	5	1	8	-22	0	-30	0	-58	-19	
Life of Crime	Counterfeiter	§760	9 p.m. –3 a.m.	Town Car	1	5	2	5	3	5	8	-22	0	-25	0	-58	-19	
Medicine	Surgeon	§700	10 p.m. –4 a.m.	Town Car	0	4	3	5	6	2	7	-22	0	-30	0	-58	-19	0
Military	Commander	§600	9 a.m. –3 p.m.	Military Jeep	1	6	5	5	5	0	5	-22	0	-33	0	-60	-25	
Politics	Judge	§650	9 a.m. –3 p.m.	Town Car	0	0	5	4	4	3	11	-22	0	-30	0	-58	-22	-1
Pro Athlete	Assistant Coach	§850	9 a.m. –2 p.m.	SUV	2	2	4	9	0	1	9	-22	0	-40	0	-70	-6	0
Science	Top Secret Researcher	§740	10 a.m. –3 p.m.	Town Car	1	6	4	0	7	4	7	-22	0	-25	0	-52	-12	-1
Xtreme	Treasure Hunter	§725	10 a.m. –5 p.m.	SUV	1	6	3	7	3	4	7	-22	0	-34	0	-60	-15	-5

Requirements for Level 9 Positions

POSITION	PAY	HOURS	CAR POOL VEHICLE	COOKING	REPAIR	CHARISMA	BODY	LOGIC	CREATIVITY	FAMILY/ FRIENDS	DAILY MOTIVE DECAY						
											HUNGER	COMFORT	HYGIENE	BLADDER	ENERGY	FUN	SOCIAL
CEO	§950	9 a.m. –4 p.m.	Limo	0	2	6	2	7	5	12	-26	0	-35	0	-62	-22	0
Broadway Star	§1100	10 a.m. –5 p.m.	Limo	0	2	8	7	0	7	12	-26	0	-35	0	-62	-22	0
Police Chief	§650	9 a.m. –5 p.m.	Limo	1	4	4	7	7	3	10	-26	0	-35	0	-62	-22	0
Smuggler	§900	9 a.m. –3 p.m.	Town Car	1	5	5	6	3	6	10	-26	0	-30	0	-62	-22	-20
Medical Researcher	§775	9 p.m. –4 a.m.	Limo	0	5	4	6	8	3	9	-26	0	-35	0	-62	-22	0
Astronaut	§625	9 a.m. –3 p.m.	Limo	1	9	5	8	6	0	9	-26	0	-35	0	-65	-30	0
Senator	§700	9 a.m. –6 p.m.	Limo	0	0	6	5	6	4	14	-26	0	-35	0	-62	-26	-15
Coach	§1,000	9 a.m. –3 p.m.	SUV	3	2	6	10	0	2	11	-26	0	-45	0	-75	-8	0
Theorist	§870	10 a.m. –2 p.m.	Town Car	1	7	4	0	9	7	8	-26	0	-30	0	-56	-16	-16
Grand Prix Driver	§825	10 a.m. –4 p.m.	Bentley	1	6	5	7	5	7	9	-26	0	-35	0	-62	-5	-10

Requirements for Level 10 Positions

POSITION	PAY	HOURS	CAR POOL VEHICLE	COOKING	REPAIR	CHARISMA	BODY	LOGIC	CREATIVITY	FAMILY/ FRIENDS	DAILY MOTIVE DECAY						
											HUNGER	COMFORT	HYGIENE	BLADDER	ENERGY	FUN	SOCIAL
Business Tycoon	§1,200	9 a.m. –3 p.m.	Limo	0	2	8	2	9	6	14	-30	0	-40	0	-66	-25	0
Superstar	§1,400	10 a.m. –3 p.m.	Limo	0	2	10	8	0	10	14	-30	0	-40	0	-66	-25	0
Captain Hero	§700	10 a.m. –4 p.m.	Limo	1	4	6	7	10	5	12	-20	-80	-45	-25	-60	0	0
Criminal Mastermind	§1,100	6 p.m. –12 a.m.	Limo	2	5	7	6	4	8	12	-30	0	-35	0	-66	-25	-25
Chief of Staff	§850	9 p.m. –4 a.m.	Hospital Limo	0	6	6	7	9	4	11	-30	0	-40	0	-66	-25	0
General	§650	9 a.m. –3 p.m.	Staff Sedan	1	10	7	10	9	0	8	-30	0	-40	0	-70	-35	0
Mayor	§750	9 a.m. –3 p.m	Limo	0	0	9	5	7	5	17	-30	0	-40	0	-66	-30	-20
Hall of Famer	§1,300	9 a.m. –3 p.m.	Limo	4	2	9	10	0	3	13	-30	0	-50	0	-80	-10	0
Mad Scientist	§1,000	10 a.m. –2 p.m.	Limo	2	8	5	0	10	10	10	-30	0	-35	0	-60	-20	-20
International	§925	11 a.m. –5 p.m.	Bentley	2	6	8	8	6	9	11	-30	0	-30	0	-70	-20	-15

The Daily Grind

A working Sim needs to follow a schedule that is conducive to good job performance. Review the following tips as you devise a work schedule for your household.

Get Plenty of Sleep

Sims need to awake refreshed in order to arrive at work in a good mood. Send your Sims to bed early, and make sure there are no distractions (stereos, TVs, computers, etc.) that might interrupt their beauty sleep.

Fig. 4-5. Make sure your Sims get to bed early enough to restore maximum Energy before the alarm rings.

Set Your Alarm Clock

When set, the clock wakes your Sims two hours before the car pool arrives (one alarm clock takes care of the entire house). This is plenty of time to take care of Hunger, Bladder, and Hygiene Motive bars. If you still have time, improve your Sim's mood with a little non-strenuous fun like watching TV, or use the extra time to improve a Skill.

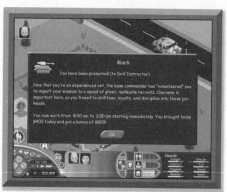

Fig. 4-6. That set on the exe bench paid of

CAUTION

If two or more Sims in the house have jobs, the alarm clock rings for the earliest riser. Unfortunately, this wakes everyone else, regardless of when they have to be ready for t car pool. If you send the other Sims back to be you'll need to wake them manually, because th alarm clock only rings once each day.

Eat a Hearty Breakfast

When you're angling for a promotion, you need arrive at work with all cylinders firing. When the alarm rings, send the designated house chef (the Sim with the highest Cooking Skill) to the kitcher "Prepare a Meal." By the time your Sim is finishe emptying his Bladder and completing necessary Hygiene, breakfast will be on the counter. There should be plenty of time to complete the meal a head to work with a full Hunger bar.

TIP

Make sure that your Sim is on the first floor and relatively close to the car pool within 15 minute of departure to be sure he or she catches his or her ride. If you meet this deadline, your Sim wil change clothes on the fly and sprint to the curb

Make Friends and Influence Your Boss

Advancing through the first three levels does not carry a friendship requirement; however this ramps up very quickly. It helps to have a stay-at-home mate to concentrate on making friends. Remember that the career friendship requirement is for your household, not your Sim. So, if your mate or children have friends, they count toward your promotions, too.

Fig. 4-7. This Sim is just about out of Energy, but his Social score is maxed out and he's just made two new friends.

Take an Occasional Day Off to Recharge

If you find that your Sim is unable to have enough Fun or Social events to maintain a positive mood, skip a day of work and indulge. See a friend or two, work on Skills, or have some Fun. Just don't miss two days in a row or your Sim will be automatically fired!

Major Decisions

As you work your way up the career ladder, you encounter "major decisions" that involve various degrees of risk. They are winner-take-all, loser-gets-nada events that force you to gamble with your salary, integrity, or even your job. The following sections include a sample "major decision" for each career.

Business

Major decision: "Stock Option"

Player is given the choice of accepting a portfolio of company stock instead of salary for that pay period. The stock could double or tank. As a result, the player receives twice his salary or nothing at all for the pay period.

Entertainment

Major decision: "The Remake"

Your agent calls with an offer: Sim Studios wants you for the lead in a remake of *Citizen Kane*. Accepting will either send your Charisma sky high when the film succeeds wildly…or send it crashing if the turkey flops.

Law Enforcement

Major decision: "The Bribe"

A mobster you're investigating offers a huge bribe to drop the case. The charges won't stick without your testimony and you *could* suddenly "lose the evidence" and quietly pocket a nice nest egg…or get busted by Internal Affairs and have to start over on a new career track.

Life of Crime

Major decision: "The Perfect Crime"

You've just been handed a hot tip that an informant claims will be an easy knockover with loads of cash for the taking. Either the tip is gold, or it's a police sting. An arrest means your family is left at home alone while you're sent off to cool your heels in Sim City Prison for a while. If you succeed, your Charisma and Creativity Skills are enhanced.

Medicine

Major Decision: "Malpractice"

A former patient has slapped you with a massive malpractice suit. You can settle immediately by offering a payment equal to 50 percent of the cash in your household account. Or, take the bum to court. Lose, and all your furniture and household goods are repossessed. Win, and you receive a settlement equal to 100 percent of the cash in your household account.

Military

Major decision: "Gung Ho"

The general needs volunteers for a highly dangerous mission. You can refuse without penalty. If you accept, and succeed on the mission, you are decorated and immediately promoted to the next level. Failure means a demotion, soldier—you're broken down to the previous level.

Politics

Major decision: "Scandal"

An attractive young member of your team also happens to be heir to a fortune. He or she will finance your career advancement if you agree to "private consultations." You can refuse, with no change in status. Otherwise, there are two possible outcomes. You might get away with it and immediately advance *two* levels. If you're caught, you'll lose your friends when the scandal breaks in the media, and you'll be tossed from the career track to seek another.

Pro Athlete

Major Decision: "The Supermatch"

A one-on-one, pay-per-view contest pitting you against your greatest local rival is offered. If you win, it's worth double your paycheck. If you lose, the indignity comes complete with an injury costing you a reduction in your Body Skill along with a drop in Charisma. The player can always refuse at no penalty.

Science

Major decision: "The Experiment"

A science research firm is willing to pay you a fat bonus for conducting a complex experiment. However, the work must be conducted at your home, using rats as test subjects. Success means you collect the fee, with a bonus increase in your Logic Skill level. A failed experiment results in a dozen rats escaping into your home. That means major bill from both your exterminator and your electrician (the rats have chewed through power cords.) Financial damage could be reduced if the Player's Repair Skills are strong.

Xtreme

Major decision: "Deep Freeze"

An arctic expedition is holding a spot open for you. It's a risky enterprise, so you may refuse. However, for a person in your particular line of work, that refusal will lower your Charisma. If you join the team, and they reach their goal, you will be rewarded with a considerable rise in Charisma. If the mission goes awry, your Sim is "lost on an iceberg" for a period of game time.

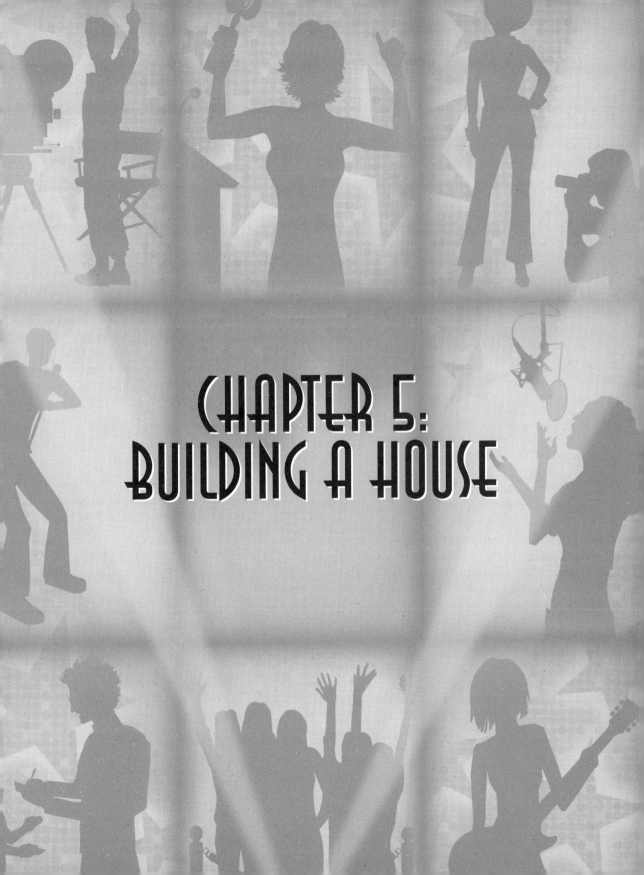

CHAPTER 5:
BUILDING A HOUSE

Introduction

Anyone who has ever built a home knows that the best laid plans of architects can sometimes turn into a house of horrors when the walls start going up. The same holds true in *The Sims*, where you have enough power to build a magnificent dream house or your worst residential nightmare. Limited only by your bank account, you can build a conservative dwelling that is functional above all else, or you can drop a family of eight in the middle of a meadow with only a bathroom and a refrigerator. It's all possible in *The Sims*, but rest assured that your family will deliver a quick—and sometimes scathing—critique when the clock starts ticking on their simulated lives.

In this chapter, we take you through the house design process from terrain preparation to landscaping. For demonstration purposes, we will use just about every building option available. Obviously, you would need a pile of Simoleans to do this in the game. However, we also cover important design considerations that enable you to maximize your Room score, regardless of your budget. In this chapter, we limit our discussion to the available options in Build Mode only. For detailed descriptions of more than 150 *Sims* objects, see the next chapter.

Of course, our suggestions are just the beginning. Sims thrive on the individuality of their creator, and if you want to build dungeons, sprawling compounds, or one-room huts, you have our support and encouragement. Remember, a bad house is no match for the bulldozer—your next house is only a click away!

TIP

Don't try to build your dream house at the beginning of the game. It's easier to tear down your original house and start over after you've fattened up your bank account.

Design Considerations

Before we introduce you to the various options available in Build Mode, here is a checklist for your basic floor plan. Invariably, your unique family of Sims will make their needs known to yo as the game progresses. However, if you follow these house design basics, you should get your family off to a positive start with a minimum of emotional outbursts.

- **Don't worry about having room to expand. Build your first house to match the number of Sims in your family.**
- **Keep the bathroom centrally located. A door on either side allows quick access for emergencies.**
- **If you start with three Sims or more, build one or more half-bathrooms (toilet and sink only) to ease the crunch.**
- **Place the house close to the street, so you don't have to do the hundred yard dash to meet your car pool.**
- **Allow enough open wall for your kitchen countertops and appliances.**
- **Make your kitchen large enough to accommodate a small table and chairs.**
- **If you don't want a separate den or family room, make one of the bedrooms large enough to handle a computer desk and chair.**

...errain Tools

...most locations you can build a roomy house on ...at piece of land without having to level the ...rain. However, if you want to build a house near ... water or at the edge of a hill, you'll need to ...ooth the sloping tiles before building a wall or ...cing an object. You can also use the Terrain ...ols to place lush, green grass over patches of dirt. ...e the pictures below for examples of each tool.

TIP

...e grid lines become noticeably darker ...hen a previously elevated or lowered terrain ...ecomes level.

Grass Tool: Simply click, hold, and drag the Grass Tool to create lawn. You can change back to dirt by holding CTRL + SHIFT and dragging the tool back over the same area.

Level Terrain: Click, hold, and drag the Level Terrain Tool to smooth out one or more tiles of land.

Lower Terrain: When you select the Lower Terrain Tool, each time you click on a tile, the terrain is lowered (so, don't hold the button down unless you want a very deep gully). This tool can have drastic effects on a landscape, so you should use it carefully, one click at a time.

Raise Terrain: The Raise Terrain Tool also works one click at a time, lifting the terrain up. If you hold down the button, the selected tile will rise quickly to its maximum height.

NOTE

Each time you use the Level, Lower, or Raise Terrain Tools, you turn any grass back into dirt. When you are finished altering the terrain, you can use the Grass Tool to quickly restore your beautiful lawn.

Wall and Fence Tools

There are several tools here, but your first step is to "frame" your house. Simply place the cursor at any tile intersection. Then click, hold, and drag to place your wall (figure 5-4). When you release the mouse button, the wood framing will change to the type of wall you selected on the Control Panel (see page 52 for descriptions of wall types).

Fig. 5-4. Drag and release to place a wall.

Although you must start a wall at an intersection, you are not limited to square walls. Simply drag the cursor at an angle to create an interesting corner (figure 5-5). However, don't make the angled walls too long. You cannot place doors, windows, or objects on these walls. Also, you cannot connect an angled wall to an existing straight wall inside your house.

Wall Tool

Wall Types

NAME	COST (PER SECTION)	DESCRIPTION
White Picket Fence	§10	Outdoor fencing
Privacy Fence	§35	8-foot outdoor fence
Monticello Balustrade	§45	Railings for balconies and stairs
Wrought Iron Balustrade	§45	Railings for balconies and stairs
Tumbleweed Wooden Column	§70	Support columns for second stories or patio covers
Wall Tool	§70	Basic unfinished wall
The Zorba Ionic Column	§80	Classic, white Graeco-Roman column
Chester Brick Column	§100	All brick, squared off column

Fig. 5-5. Angled corners help you transform a boring box into a custom home.

Door and Window Tools

Door Tool

Sims are very active. They seek the best path for their current task, and they think nothing of going out one exterior door and back in through another, if it's the best route. The least expensive Walnut Door (figure 5-6) is only §100, but because is solid, your Room score does not benefit from outside light. If at all possible, invest in one of the windowed doors, and ideally, pick the multi-paned Monticello Door for maximum light.

Fig. 5-6. The Walnut Door gives your Sims privacy, but it doesn't allow outside light to improve your Room score.

Door Types

NAME	COST	NOTES
Walnut Door	§100	Solid door without windows
Maple Door Frame	§150	Wooden door frame for rooms that do not require total privacy
Federal Lattice Window Door	§200	Glass panes in the upper half of door
Windsor Door	§300	Designer leaded glass door
Monticello Door	§400	7 rows of 3 panes, topped with a 6-pane half circle, allow maximum light to flow into your home

Window Tool

Let the sun shine in to pump up your Room score. Sims love light, so install plenty of windows from the start. Simply click on the selected window and place it on any right-angle wall (remember, you cannot place doors, windows, or objects on a diagonal wall). Window style is strictly personal—all windows exert the same positive effect on the Room score.

TIP

For aesthetic value, match your windows to your door style, such as the Monticello Door with Monticello Windows, as pictured in figure 5-7.

Fig. 5-7. Monticello Doors and Windows provide maximum light.

Window Types

NAME	COST	DESCRIPTION
Single-Pane Fixed Window	§50	This economy window still lets in the sun.
Single-Hung Window	§55	This looks good over the kitchen sink.
Privacy Window	§60	Tired of the neighborhood peeping Toms? This window is positioned higher on the wall.
Plate Glass Window	§65	This one's strictly glass from floor to ceiling.
El Sol Window	§80	This round ornamental window is a nice change from square and rectangular styles.
Monticello Window	§110	Use as a bedroom window to complement the Monticello door.
Windsor Window	§120	This ornamental natural wood window adds turn-of-the-century character to your home.
Monticello Window Full-Length	§200	This dramatic window looks beautiful on either side of a Monticello door.

Floor Tool

Unless you like grass in your living room, use the Floor Tool to lay some flooring inside your hous *The Sims* also includes outdoor flooring that wo well in patios, backyard barbecue areas, or as pathways to a pool or play area. One tile covers single grid, and you can quickly finish an entire room with a single shift-click. The price range fo floor coverings is §10–§20, and you have a selection of 29 different styles/colors.

TIP

When you lay flooring inside a room with angled walls, half of the floor tiles appear on the other side of the wall, in another room or outside the house (see figure 5-8). To remove these outside tiles, place any floor type over th tiles, hold down the Ctrl *key, and then click to delete them. The flooring on the other side of the wall remains undisturbed.*

Fig. 5-8. After y finish the inside flooring, go bac and delete the external tiles.

NOTE

You can use any type of flooring inside or outside.

Flooring Types

- Carpeting (7)
- Cement (1)
- Ceramic Tile-Small Tiles (3)
- Checkerboard Linoleum (1)
- Clay Paver Tiles (1)
- Colored Pavement (1)
- Granite (2)
- Gravel (1)
- Hardwood Plank (1)
- Inlaid Hardwood (1)
- Italian Tile (1)
- Poured Concrete (1)
- Shale (1)
- Striped Pavement (2, Both Directions)
- Tatami Mats (2)
- Terracotta Tile (1)
- Wood Parquet (2)

Wallpaper Tool

Fig. 5-9. Use the Wallpaper Tool to create a different mood in every room.

There are 30 different indoor/outdoor wall coverings in *The Sims,* and just as with floor coverings, you are limited only by your budget and sense of style. Prices range from §4 for basic wallpaper to §14 for granite block. If you change your mind after putting up the wallpaper, you can rip it down and get your money back by holding down the [Ctrl] key and clicking on the ugly panel.

Wallpaper Types

- Adobe (1)
- Aluminum Siding (1)
- Brick (2)
- Granite (1)
- Interior Wall Treatments (6 Fabric and Paint Combinations)
- Japanese Paper/Screens (4)
- Paint (4)
- Plaster (1)
- Stucco (1)
- Tudor (1)
- Wainscoting (1)
- Wallpaper (4)
- Wood Clapboard (1)
- Wood Paneling (1)
- Wood Shingles (1)

Stair Tool

You may not plan to build a second story immediately, but it's still a good idea to place your staircase before you start filling your house with objects. Choose from four staircases, two at §900 and two at §1,200. But, no matter how much you spend, they still get your Sims up and down the same way.

Style is considerably less important than function. You don't want to interrupt the traffic flow inside your house, especially to critical rooms such as the bathroom and kitchen. For this reason, staircases work well against a wall, where they are out of the way, or between two large, open rooms, such as the kitchen and family room (figure 5-10).

Fig. 5-10. Both of these placements keep the staircases out of the main traffic patterns.

If you don't have the money to finish the second story, just place the staircase and forget about it. The Sims won't go upstairs until you add a second story. After the staircase is positioned, the process for building a second story is exactly the same as building the first floor. The only obvious difference is that the buildable wall space extends out one square beyond the walls on the first floor. This allows you to squeeze a little extra space for a larger room or balcony.

Roof Tool

Although it is much easier to play The Sims using the Walls Cutaway or Walls Down options on the Control Panel, you will want to step back and enjoy your masterpiece in all of its crowning glory. The Roof Tool allows you to select a Shallow, Medium, or Steep Pitch for your roof, and choose from a selection of four roof patterns.

Water Tools
Pool Tool

Now that you have walls, floors, and doors, it's time to add a pool. Of course, this isn't a necess but your Sims love to swim, and it's an easy way add important Body points. After placing your pool, don't forget to add a ladder so your Sims get in and out of the pool (diving board is optional). The Pool Tool also places light-colored cement squares as decking around your pool. Yo can go back and cover these tiles with the outdc surface of your choice, as displayed in figure 5-1 You can also add fencing around your deck to gi your pool a more finished look.

Fig. 5-11. With pool and deckir place, you have room to add an outdoor barbec and beverage c

ater Tool

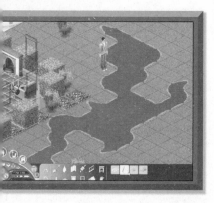

Fig. 5-12.

ou want to add decorative, free form pools on
r property, use the Water Tool to place oval-
ped sections of pond. You can drag the tool to
ce a long oval pond, or connect several small
nds to form an irregular pattern, as pictured in
ure 5-12. Your Sims can't swim in ponds, and
y cannot walk on water, so don't forget to
ude a pathway.

replace Tool

Fig. 5-13. It looks
innocent enough,
but a roaring fire
can turn nearby
objects or Sims into
a deadly inferno.

en placed safely out of the way of flammable
ects, a fireplace adds a major boost to the
m score. However, it can be a dangerous fire
ard if Sims wander too close, so give it a wide
h when a fire is roaring.

Plant Tool

Now, it's time to put the finishing touches on the
exterior of your house. Using the Plant Tool, you
can select from 14 different plants, priced from §5
for Wildflowers to §300 for an Apple Tree. The
following types of vegetation are included:

Plant Types

- **Flowers (4)**
- **Bushes (1)**
- **Hedges (2)**
- **Shrubs (2)**
- **Trees (5)**

Let your green thumb go wild, but don't forget
that only trees and shrubs will thrive without
regular watering. If you want colorful flowers,
you'll probably need to hire a Gardener.

Fig. 5-14. This
colorful landscaping
will require the
services of a
Gardener, or a Sim
with a lot of time
to kill.

Special Editing Tools

In addition to the building tools described above, there are two other options on the Build Mode Control Panel. The curved arrows pictured at the bottom corner of figure 5-15 allow you to undo or repeat your last action(s). This is a quick way to delete unwanted items.

Fig. 5-15. Click Undo Last to reverse your most recent actions.

If the undo button is unavailable, you can clic on the Hand Tool, select any object, and then pre the Delete key to sell it back. For directions on h to delete walls, wall coverings, and floor coverin see the appropriate sections in this chapter.

Fig. 5-16. Selec item with the ⬧ Tool, then press Delete to make go away.

CHAPTER 6:
MATERIAL SIMS

Introduction

This chapter covers the eight categories of objects available in Buy Mode: Seating, Surfaces, Decorative, Electronics, Appliances, Plumbing, Lighting, and Miscellaneous. Every object is listed with its purchase price, related Motives, and Efficiency ratings. You can shop 'til you drop, but it's more important to buy smart than to buy often. Our comprehensive Buying Guide is just ahead, but first let's study some important factors that impact your spending habits.

Buying for Needs, Instead of Needing to Buy

If you select a ready-made house for your new Sim family, you acquire walls, floors, and a roof, but little else. The house is empty, with nary a toilet, bed, or refrigerator in sight. Depending upon how much you spent on the house, you'll have a few thousand Simoleans to use in Buy Mode, where you can purchase more than 150 objects. Most objects affect your Sims' environment in positive ways. However, not every object is a necessity. In fact, if you are a recovering shopping channel addict, this is not a good time to fall off your wallet. Make your first purchases with The Sims' Motives (or Needs) in mind. You can review your Sims' current Needs state by clicking on the Mood icon. We provide detailed descriptions in the Motives chapter, but for now, here is a basic shopping list that will help you get your Sims' Need bars out of the red zone during the early stages of a game.

TIP

In most instances, an expensive item has a greater impact on the related Need bar than an economy model. For example, a §300 cot gives your Sim a place to crash, but a §3,000 Mission Bed provides more Comfort and lets your Sim get by on less sleep. As an added bonus, the top-of-the-line bed also adds to the overall Room score.

Fig. 6-1. Despite logging only f[...] hours of sleep, [...] is feeling pret[...] good, thanks t[...] §3000 Mission [...]

Fig. 6-2. A big-screen TV is fu[...] your Sims, but [...] for the neighb[...] who will often [...] out, and boost [...] Social score.

ED	ITEM	EXPLANATION
unger	Refrigerator, Food Processor, Stove	A refrigerator alone will sustain life, but you will greatly improve the quality of Sim meals by using a food processor and stove. However, there is a risk of fire if your Sim doesn't have at least two Cooking Skill points.
omfort	Bed, Chairs	Sims will sleep anywhere when they are tired, but a bed is highly recommended for sleeping, and you'll need chairs (for eating and working at the computer), and a couch for napping. A bathtub provides a little extra comfort for your Sims, but it isn't critical, provided you have a shower.
ygiene	Sink, Shower	Dirty Sims spend a lot of time waving their arms in the air to disperse their body odor. Not a pretty sight. Fortunately, a sink and shower go a long way toward improving their state of mind (not to mention the smell).
adder	Toilet	When you gotta go, you gotta go. Sims prefer using a toilet, but if one is not available, they will relieve themselves on the floor. This not only causes great shame and embarrassment, but someone in your family will have to clean up the mess. It's also very bad for your Hygiene levels.
ergy	Bed	If you don't want to spawn a family of insomniacs, buy a sufficient number of beds for your Sims. A shot of coffee or espresso provides a temporary Energy boost, but it is definitely not a long-term solution.
n	TV	The boob tube is the easiest and cheapest way to give your Sims a break from their daily grinds. You can add other, more exciting, items later, but this is your best choice early on.
cial	Telephone	Ignore this for a short time while you focus on setting up your house. However, don't force your Sims into a solitary lifestyle. Other Sims may walk by the house, but you'll have better results after buying a telephone, so that you can invite people over and gain Social points when they arrive.
om	Windows, Lamps, Decorations, Landscaping	Sims like plenty of light, from windows during the day and artificial lighting at night. Table Lamps are the cheapest, but they can only be placed on raised surfaces. As your game progresses, you can add decorations and landscaping to boost the Room score.

ms Can Be Hard to Please

en a fat bank account, it would seem that you can always cheer up your Sims with a few expensive chases. Not exactly. While you are spending your hard-earned Simoleans, the Sims are busy paring everything that you buy to everything they already own. If you fail to keep your Sims in the ner to which they are accustomed, their responses to your new objects may be indifferent or even nright negative. Every time you make a purchase, the game uses an assessment formula to calculate Sim's response. The logic goes like this:

- Calculates the average value of everything in your house (including outdoor items).

- Subtracts 10 percent of the new object's value for each existing copy of the same item. Don't expect your family members to jump for joy if you add a hot tub to every room in the house.

- Compares the value of the new object with all existing objects in your house. If the new purchase is worth 20 percent or more above the average value of current items, the Sim exhibits a positive response by clapping.

- If the new object is within 20 percent (above or below) of the current average value of all items in your household, the Sim gives you an uninspired shrug.

- If the new object is less than 20 percent below the average value, your Sim waves it off and you'll see a red X through the object.

Your Diminishing Net Wor

When times are tough, you may need to raise cash by selling objects in your house. With rare exception, you will never match your initial investment, thanks to instant depreciation, and as time goes on, your belongings continue to lo value until they reach their depreciation limits. The following table lists every object in *The Sim* (alphabetically), including purchase price and depreciated values.

TIP

Although depreciation reduces the value of your furnishings over time, there is a buyer's remorse period when you can return the item for full value (if it has been less than 24 hours since you purchased it). So, if you have second thoughts about that new hot tub, simply sele the item and hit the Delete key to get your money back.

Fig. 6-3. Compared to the §2,100 "Snails With Icicles in Nose," this §45 clown picture doesn't quite stack up.

Fig. 6-4. This Pyrotorre Gas Range is §1,0 new, but after depreciation i worth only §3

...ect Depreciation

...AME	PURCHASE PRICE	INITIAL DEPRECIATION	DAILY DEPRECIATION	DEPRECIATION LIMIT
...larm: Burglar	§250	§62	§2	§50
...larm: Smoke	§50	§12	§0	§10
...quarium	§200	§30	§2	§80
...ar	§800	§120	§8	§320
...arbecue	§350	§70	§4	§105
...asketball Hoop (...heap Eaze)	§650	§98	§6	§260
...ed: Double	§450	§68	§4	§180
...ed: Double (Mission)	§3,000	§450	§30	§1,200
...ed: Double (Napoleon)	§1,000	§150	§10	§400
...ed: Single (Spartan)	§300	§45	§3	§120
...ed: Single (Tyke Nyte)	§450	§68	§4	§180
...ench: Garden	§250	§38	§2	§100
...ookshelf: Amishim	§500	§75	§5	§200
...ookshelf: Libri di Regina	§900	§135	§9	§360
...ookshelf: Pine	§250	§38	§2	§100
...hair: Deck (Survivall)	§150	§22	§2	§60
...hair: Dining (Empress)	§600	§90	§6	§240
...hair: Dining (...arisienne)	§1,200	§180	§12	§480
...hair: Dining (Teak)	§200	§30	§2	§80
...hair: Dining (...erkbunnst)	§80	§12	§1	§32
...hair: Living Room (...itronel)	§450	§68	§4	§180
...hair: Living Room (...ountry Class)	§250	§38	§2	§100
...hair: Living Room (...arrbach)	§500	§75	§5	§200
...hair: Living Room (...icker)	§80	§12	§1	§32
...air: Office	§100	§15	§1	§40

NAME	PURCHASE PRICE	INITIAL DEPRECIATION	DAILY DEPRECIATION	DEPRECIATION LIMIT
Chair: Recliner (Back Slack)	§250	§38	§2	§100
Chair: Recliner (Von Braun)	§850	§128	§8	§340
Chess Set	§500	§75	§5	§200
Clock: Alarm	§30	§4	§0	§12
Clock: Grandfather	§3,500	§525	§35	§1,400
Coffee: Espresso Machine	§450	§90	§4	§135
Coffeemaker	§85	§17	§1	§26
Computer (Brahma 2000)	§2,800	§700	§28	§560
Computer (Marco)	§6,500	§1,625	§65	§1,300
Computer (Microscotch)	§1,800	§450	§18	§360
Computer (Moneywell)	§999	§250	§10	§200
Counter: Bath (Count Blanc)	§400	§60	§4	§160
Counter: Kitchen (Barcelona: In)	§800	§120	§8	§320
Counter: Kitchen (Barcelona: Out)	§800	§120	§8	§320
Counter: Kitchen (NuMica)	§150	§22	§2	§60
Counter: Kitchen (Tiled)	§250	§38	§2	§100
Desk (Cupertino)	§220	§33	§2	§88
Desk (Mesquite)	§80	§12	§1	§32
Desk (Redmond)	§800	§120	§8	§320
Dishwasher (Dish Duster)	§550	§110	§6	§165
Dishwasher (Fuzzy Logic)	§950	§190	§10	§285
Dollhouse	§180	§27	§2	§72
Dresser (Antique Armoire)	§1,200	§180	§12	§480
Dresser (Kinderstuff)	§300	§45	§3	§120

ME	PURCHASE PRICE	INITIAL DEPRECIATION	DAILY DEPRECIATION	DEPRECIATION LIMIT
esser (Oak Armoire)	§550	§82	§6	§220
esser (Pinegulcher)	§250	§38	§2	§100
sel	§250	§38	§2	§100
ercise Machine	§700	§105	§7	§280
amingo	§12	§2	§0	§5
od Processor	§220	§44	§2	§66
untain	§700	§105	§7	§280
idge (Freeze Secret)	§2,500	§500	§25	§750
idge (Llamark)	§600	§120	§6	§180
idge (Porcina)	§1,200	§240	§12	§360
ot Tub	§6,500	§1,300	§65	§1,950
mp: Floor (Halogen)	§50	§8	§0	§20
mp: Floor (Lumpen)	§100	§15	§1	§40
mp: Floor (orchosteronne)	§350	§52	§4	§140
mp: Garden	§50	§7	§1	§20
mp: Love n' Haight ava	§80	§12	§1	§32
mp: Table (Antique)	§300	§45	§3	§120
mp: Table (Bottle)	§25	§4	§0	§10
mp: Table (Ceramiche)	§85	§13	§1	§34
mp: Table (Elite)	§180	§27	§2	§72
edicine Cabinet	§125	§19	§1	§50
icrowave	§250	§50	§2	§75
irror: Floor	§150	§22	§2	§60
irror: Wall	§100	§15	§1	§40
one: Tabletop	§50	§12	§0	§10
one: Wall	§75	§19	§1	§15
ano	§3,500	§525	§35	§1,400
nball Machine	§1,800	§450	§18	§360
ant: Big (Cactus)	§150	§22	§2	§60
ant: Big (Jade)	§160	§24	§2	§64
ant: Big (Rubber)	§120	§18	§1	§48

NAME	PURCHASE PRICE	INITIAL DEPRECIATION	DAILY DEPRECIATION	DEPRECIATION LIM
Plant: Small (Geranium)	§45	§7	§0	§18
Plant: Small (Spider)	§35	§5	§0	§14
Plant: Small (Violets)	§30	§4	§0	§12
Play Structure	§1,200	§180	§12	§480
Pool Table	§4,200	§630	§42	§1,680
Shower	§650	§130	§6	§195
Sink: Bathroom Pedestal	§400	§80	§4	§120
Sink: Kitchen (Double)	§500	§100	§5	§150
Sink: Kitchen (Single)	§250	§50	§2	§75
Sofa (Blue Pinstripe)	§400	§60	§4	§160
Sofa (Contempto)	§200	§30	§2	§80
Sofa (Country)	§450	§68	§4	§180
Sofa (Deiter)	§1,100	§165	§11	§440
Sofa (Dolce)	§1,450	§218	§14	§580
Sofa (Recycled)	§180	§27	§2	§72
Sofa (SimSafari)	§220	§33	§2	§88
Sofa: Loveseat (Blue Pinstripe)	§360	§54	§4	§144
Sofa: Loveseat (Contempto)	§150	§22	§2	§60
Sofa: Loveseat (Country)	§340	§51	§3	§136
Sofa: Loveseat (Indoor-Outdoor)	§160	§24	§2	§64
Sofa: Loveseat (Luxuriare)	§875	§131	§9	§350
Stereo (Strings)	§2,550	§638	§26	§510
Stereo (Zimantz)	§650	§162	§6	§130
Stereo: Boom Box	§100	§25	§1	§20
Stove (Dialectric)	§400	§80	§4	§120
Stove (Pyrotorre)	§1,000	§200	§10	§300
Table: Dining (Colonial)	§200	§30	§2	§80
Table: Dining (Mesa)	§450	§68	§4	§180

...ME	PURCHASE PRICE	INITIAL DEPRECIATION	DAILY DEPRECIATION	DEPRECIATION LIMIT
...le: Dining (NuMica)	§95	§14	§1	§38
...le: Dining (...risienne)	§1,200	§180	§12	§480
...le: End (Anywhere)	§120	§18	§1	§48
...le: End (Imperious)	§135	§20	§1	§54
...le: End (KinderStuff)	§75	§11	§1	§30
...le: End (Mission)	§250	§38	§2	§100
...le: End (Pinegulcher)	§40	§6	§0	§16
...le: End (Sumpto)	§300	§45	§3	§120
...le: End (Wicker)	§55	§8	§1	§22
...le: Outdoor (...ackwoods)	§200	§30	§2	§80
...aster Oven	§100	§20	§1	§30
...ilet (Flush Force)	§1,200	§240	§12	§360
...ilet (Hygeia-O-Matic)	§300	§60	§3	§90
...mbstone/Urn	§5	§1	§0	§2
...y Box	§50	§8	§0	§20
...ain Set: Large	§955	§239	§10	§191
...ain Set: Small	§80	§20	§1	§16
...sh Compactor	§375	§75	§4	§112
...b (Hydrothera)	§3,200	§640	§32	§960
...b (Justa)	§800	§160	§8	§240
...b (Sani-Queen)	§1,500	§300	§15	§450
... (Monochrome)	§85	§21	§1	§17
... (Soma)	§3,500	§875	§35	§700
... (Trottco)	§500	§125	§5	§100
... Glasses	§2,300	§575	§23	§460

The Sims Buying Guide

The following sections represent the eight item categories that appear when you click the Buy Mode button on the control panel. We've added a few subcategories to make it easier to find a specific object. The Efficiency Value (1–10) indicates how well the item satisfies each Motive. You get what you pay for in *The Sims*, so an §80 chair doesn't quite stack up to an §850 recliner when it comes to boosting your Comfort level, and it cannot restore Energy.

Seating

Chairs

There are three types of chairs in *The Sims*: movable, stationary, and reclining. Any chair will function at a desk or table for eating and using objects. If your budget is tight, you can also use cheaper chairs for watching TV or reading, but their Comfort ratings are very low. You can use high-ticket dining room chairs at the computer, but that is probably overkill. You are better off placing them in the dining room where you receive greater benefit from their enhanced Room ratings.

Stationary chairs are cushier and nicely upholstered (depending on your taste, of course), and they usually provide more comfort. Finally, the reclining chairs are top of the line, giving you increased comfort and the added benefit of being able to catch a few Zs in the reclining position.

> ## TIP
> *Chair placement is critical, especially around tables. A Sim will not move a chair sideways, only forward and backward. So, position the chair properly or the Sim will not be able to u the table (or what is on it). Also, be careful n to trap a Sim in a corner when a chair is pulle out. For example, if a child is playing with a train set in the corner of the room, and anoth Sim pulls out a chair to use the computer, the child would be trapped in the corner until the computer user is finished.*

Werkbunnst All-Purpose Chair

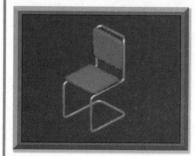

Type: Movable

Cost: §80

Motive: Comfort (2)

Posture Plus Office Chair

Type: Movable

Cost: §100

Motive: Comfort (3)

...ck Chair by Survivall

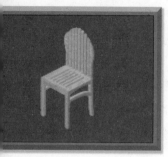

Type: Movable

Cost: §150

Motive: Comfort (3)

Parisienne Dining Chair

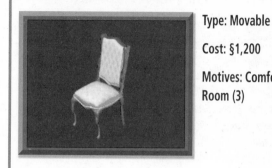

Type: Movable

Cost: §1,200

Motives: Comfort (6), Room (3)

...ch of Teak Dinette Chair

Type: Movable

Cost: §200

Motive: Comfort (3)

Sioux City Wicker Chair

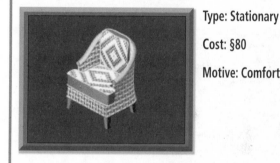

Type: Stationary

Cost: §80

Motive: Comfort (2)

...press Dining Room Chair

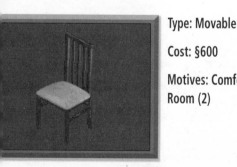

Type: Movable

Cost: §600

Motives: Comfort (4), Room (2)

Country Class Armchair

Type: Stationary

Cost: §250

Motive: Comfort (4)

"Citronel" from Chiclettina Inc.

Type: Stationary

Cost: §450

Motive: Comfort (6)

"The Sarrbach" by Werkbunnst

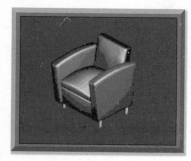

Type: Stationary

Cost: §500

Motive: Comfort (6)

"Back Slack" Recliner

Type: Recliner

Cost: §250

Motives: Comfort (6), Energy (3)

"Von Braun" Recliner

Type: Recliner

Cost: §850

Motives: Comfort (9), Energy (3)

Couches

Sitting down is fine for reading, eating, or working, but for serious vegging, your Sims nee good couch. When selecting a couch, function i more important than quality. If you are looking a place to take naps, pay more attention to the Energy rating than the Comfort or Room rating multipurpose couch should have good Energy a Comfort ratings. However, if you are furnishing your party area, select one that looks good, thereby enhancing your Room rating. Stay away from the cheapest couches (under §200). For a f extra dollars, a medium-priced couch will make your Sims a lot happier. When you're flush with Simoleans, don't forget to dress up your garden with the outdoor bench. You can't sleep on it, b it looks great.

Contempto Loveseat

Cost: §150

Motives: Comfort (3), Energy (4)

or-Outdoor Loveseat

Cost: §160

Motives: Comfort (3), Energy (4)

SimSafari Sofa

Cost: §220

Motives: Comfort (3), Energy (5)

ycled Couch

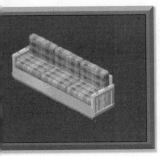

Cost: §180

Motives: Comfort (2), Energy (5)

Parque Fresco del Aire Bench

Cost: §250

Motive: Comfort (2)

tempto Couch

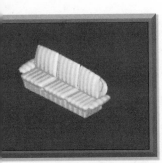

Cost: §200

Motives: Comfort (3), Energy (5)

Country Class Loveseat

Cost: §340

Motives: Comfort (5), Energy (4)

Pinstripe Loveseat from Zecutime

Cost: §360

Motives: Comfort (5), Energy (4)

Pinstripe Sofa from Zecutime

Cost: §400

Motives: Comfort (5), Energy (5)

Country Class Sofa

Cost: §450

Motives: Comfort (5), Energy (5)

Luxuriare Loveseat

Cost: §875

Motives: Comfort (8), Energy (4), Room (2)

"The Deiter" by Werkbunnst

Cost: §1,100

Motives: Comfort (8), Energy (5), Room (3)

Dolce Tutti Frutti Sofa

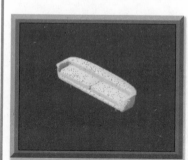

Cost: §1,450

Motives: Comfort (9), Energy (5), Room (3)

...ing enough sleep can be one of the most ...rating goals in *The Sims*, especially if there is ...w baby in the house, or your car pool arrives ...me ungodly hour of the morning. In the early ...es of a game, it is not important to spend a ...dle of money on a designer bed. However, an ...ade later on is well worth the money, ...use a top-of-the-line bed recharges your ...gy bar faster.

Tyke Nyte Bed

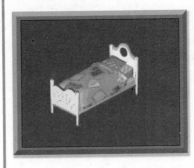

Cost: §450

Motives: Comfort (7), Energy (7)

...tan Special

Cost: §300

Motives: Comfort (6), Energy (7)

Napoleon Sleigh Bed

Cost: §1,000

Motives: Comfort (8), Energy (9)

...p Eazzzzze Double Sleeper

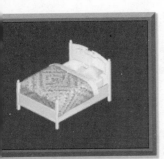

Cost: §450

Motives: Comfort (7), Energy (8)

Modern Mission Bed

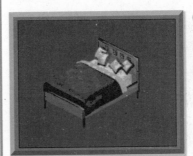

Cost: §3,000

Motives: Comfort (9), Energy (10), Room (3)

Surfaces

Sims will eat or read standing up if they have to, but they won't be particularly happy about it. Sitting at a table while eating a meal bolsters a Sim's Comfort. Since your Sims have to eat to satisfy Hunger, they might as well improve Comfort, too. Many objects require elevated surfaces, so allow enough room for nightstands (alarm clock, lamps), tables (computer), and countertops (microwave, coffeemaker, etc.), when you design the interior of your house. Also, your Sims cannot prepare food on a table, so provide ample countertop space in the kitchen, or you may find them wandering into the bathroom to chop veggies on the counter (hair in the soup—yummy!).

Countertops

NuMica Kitchen Counter

Cost: §150

Motive: None

Tiled Counter

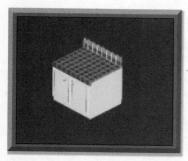

Cost: §250

Motive: None

Count Blanc Bathroom Counter

Cost: §400

Motive: None

"Barcelona" Outcurve Counter

Cost: §800

Motive: Room (2)

"Barcelona" Incurve Counter

Cost: §800

Motive: Room (2)

Tables

gulcher End Table

Cost: §40

Motive: None

ker Breeze End Table

Cost: §55

Motive: None

ywhere" End Table

Cost: §120

Motive: None

Imperious Island End Table

Cost: §135

Motive: None

Modern Mission End Table

Cost: §250

Motive: Room (1)

Sumpto End Table

Cost: §300

Motive: Room (1)

KinderStuff Nightstand

Cost: §75

Motive: None

Desks/Tables

Mesquite Desk/Table

Cost: §80

Motive: None

NuMica Folding Card Table

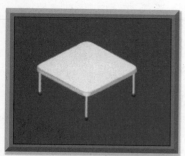

Cost: §95

Motive: None

"Colonial Legacy" Dining Table

Cost: §200

Motive: None

Backwoods Table by Survivall

Cost: §200

Motive: None

London "Cupertino" Collection Desk/Table

Cost: §220

Motive: None

lon "Mesa" Dining Design

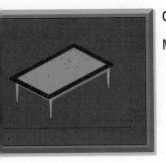

Cost: §450

Motive: Room (2)

"Redmond" Desk/Table

Cost: §800

Motive: Room (2)

isienne Dining Table

Cost: §1,200

Motive: Room (3)

Decorative

After the essential furnishings are in place, you can improve your Room score by adding decorative objects. Some items, such as the grandfather clock and aquarium, require regular maintenance, but most decorative items exist solely for your Sims' viewing pleasure. You might even get lucky and buy a painting or sculpture that increases in value. In addition to enhancing the Room score, the aquarium and fountain have Fun value.

Pink Flamingo

Cost: §12

Motive: Room (2)

African Violet

Cost: §30

Motive: Room (1)

Spider Plant

Cost: §35

Motive: Room (1)

Watercolor by J.M.E.

Cost: §75

Motive: Room (1)

"Roxana" Geranium

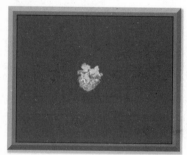

Cost: §45

Motive: Room (1)

Rubber Tree Plant

Cost: §120

Motive: Room (2)

"Tragic Clown" Painting

Cost: §45

Motive: Room (1)

Echinopsis maximus Cactus

Cost: §150

Motive: Room (2)

Plant

Cost: §160

Motive: Room (2)

"Delusion de Grandeur"

Cost: §360

Motive: Room (2)

eidon's Adventure Aquarium

Cost: §200

Motive: Fun (1), Room (2)

"Fountain of Tranquility"

Cost: §700

Motives: Fun (1), Room (2)

-Polar" by Conner I.N.

Cost: §240

Motive: Room (2)

Landscape #12,001 by Manny Kopees

Cost: §750

Motive: Room (3)

Bust of Athena by Klassick Repro. Inc.

Cost: §875

Motive: Room (3)

"Scylla and Charybdis"

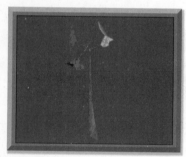

Cost: §1,450

Motive: Room (4)

Snails With Icicles in Nose

Cost: §2,140

Motive: Room (5)

Portrait Grid by Payne A. Pitcher

Cost: §3,200

Motive: Room (8)

Grandfather Clock

Cost: §3,500

Motive: Room (7)

Blue China Vase

Cost: §4,260

Motive: Room (7)

ll Life, Drapery and Crumbs"

Cost: §7,600

Motive: Room (9)

rge Black Slab" by ChiChi Smith

Cost: §12,648

Motive: Room (10)

ectronics

s game offers a veritable potpourri of high-tech dgetry, ranging from potentially lifesaving items h as smoke detectors to nonessential purchases h as pinball games or virtual reality headsets. yond the critical electronics items—smoke tectors, telephone for receiving calls or calling vices and friends, TV for cheap fun, and mputer for finding a job—you should focus on ms with group activity potential, especially if u like socializing and throwing parties.

TIP

Electronic items can break down on a regular basis, so it is a good idea to bone up on Mechanical Skills. Until you have a qualified fix-it Sim in the house, you'll be shelling out §50 an hour for a repairman.

FireBrand Smoke Detector

Cost: §50

Motive: None

Notes: Each detector covers one room. At the very least, place a detector in any room that has a stove or fireplace.

SimSafety IV Burglar Alarm

Cost: §250

Motive: None

Notes: An alarm unit covers one room, but an outside alarm covers an area within five tiles of the house. The police are called immediately when the alarm goes off.

SCTC BR-8 Standard Telephone

Cost: §50

Motive: None

Notes: This phone needs a surface, so it's less accessible. Best location is in the kitchen; stick with wall phones in the rest of the house.

SCTC Cordless Wall Phone

Cost: §75

Motive: None

Notes: Place these phones wherever your Sims spend a lot of time.

Urchineer Train Set by Rip Co.

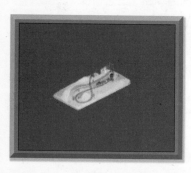

Cost: §80

Motive: Fun (2)

Notes: Group activity; can only be used by kids.

Televisions

Buying a TV is the easiest way to put a little fun into your Sims' lives, and it is a group activity. You can maximize the effect by matching the program category with your Sim's personality, as noted in the following table.

PERSONALITY	FAVORITE TV SHOW
Active	Action
Grouchy (low nice)	Horror
Outgoing	Romance
Playful	Cartoon

Your TV will eventually break down, especially if you have a family of couch potatoes. Do not attempt to repair the TV unless your Sim has at least one Mechanical Skill point (three is even better). If your Sim doesn't have the proper training, poking around inside the TV will result in electrocution.

Monochrome TV

Cost: §85

Motive: Fun (2)

Notes: Strictly for tight budgets, but it gives your Sims a little mindless fun.

.tco 27" Color Television B94U

Cost: §500

Motive: Fun (4)

es: A lazy Sim's favorite activity is watching TV.

.a Plasma TV

Cost: §3,500

Motive: Fun (6), Room (2)

es: It's expensive, but it provides instant entertainment for a
house.

.reos

.ncing to the music is a great group activity,
.ecially for Sims with effervescent personalities
.though it is perfectly acceptable to dance
.ne). When a Sim dances with a houseguest, it
.reases both their Fun and Social ratings. You
. personalize *The Sims* by placing your own MP3
.s in the Music/Stations directory.

"Down Wit Dat" Boom Box

Cost: §100

Motive: Fun (2)

Notes: An inexpensive way to start a party in your front yard.

Zimantz Component Hi-Fi Stereo

Cost: §650

Motive: Fun (3)

Notes: Perfect for your big party room.

Strings Theory Stereo

Cost: §2,550

Motives: Fun (5), Room (3)

Notes: The ultimate party machine, this is the only stereo that
enhances your Room score.

Computers

A computer is a Sim's best tool for finding a job. The computer has three job postings every day, making it three times as productive as the newspaper employment ads. Aside from career search, the computer provides entertainment for the entire family, and it helps the kids keep their grades up (better chance of cash rewards from the grandparents). Playful and lazy Sims love the computer. However, if only serious Sims occupy your house, you can grab a newspaper and let the age of technology pass you by.

Moneywell Computer

Cost: §999

Motive: Fun (3), Study

Notes: All you need is a basic computer for job searching.

Microscotch Covetta Q628-1500JA

Cost: §1,800

Motive: Fun (5), Study

Notes: More power translates into better gaming.

The Brahma 2000

Cost: §2,800

Motive: Fun (7), Study

Notes: More than twice the fun of a basic computer.

Meet Marco

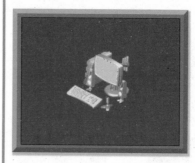

Cost: §6,500

Motive: Fun (9), Study

Notes: For Sim power users—the family will fight for playing time on this beast.

Games

OCD Systems SimRailRoad Town

Cost: §955

Motive: Fun (4), Room (

Notes: You need a large area for this train table, but it is an excell group activity and it gives a serious boost to your Room score.

Me, Feel Me" Pinball Machine

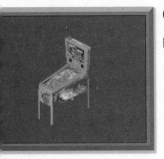

Cost: §1,800

Motive: Fun (5)

s: Build a big family room and add a pinball machine to
your guests occupied for hours.

Virtual Reality Set

Cost: §2,300

Motive: Fun (7)

s: Playful Sims have been known to don VR glasses on their
to the bathroom (even with full bladders). For grins, wait
a Sim puts on the glasses, then immediately issue another
nand. The Sim head on the control panel will wear the
es for the duration of your game.

pliances

h the exception of the dishwasher and trash
npactor, the Sim appliances are all devoted to
creation of food or java. At a bare minimum,
need refrigeration. However, if you want your
s to eat like royalty, train at least one family
mber in the gentle art of cooking and provide
t Sim with the latest in culinary tools.

Mr. Regular-Joe Coffee

Cost: §85

Motive: Bladder (-1),
Energy (1)

Notes: Only adults can partake of the coffee rush. The effects
are temporary, but sometimes it's the only way to get rolling.

Gagmia Simore Espresso Machine

Cost: §450

Motive: Bladder (-2),
Energy (2), Fun (1)

Notes: If you want a morning jolt, espresso is the way to go.
You'll fill your bladder twice as fast as with regular coffee, but it
is a small price to pay for more energy and a splash of fun.

Brand Name Toaster Oven

Cost: §100

Motive: Hunger (1)

Notes: This little roaster is better at starting fires than cooking food. Improve your Cooking Skills and buy a real oven. Until then, use a microwave.

Positive Potential Microwave

Cost: §250

Motive: Hunger (2)

Notes: You can warm up your food without burning the house down.

Dialectric Free Standing Range

Cost: §400

Motive: Hunger (5)

Notes: After raising your Cooking Skills to three or above, you can create nutritious (and satisfying) meals on this stove.

The "Pyrotorre" Gas Range

Cost: §1,000

Motive: Hunger (7)

Notes: A skilled chef can create works of art on this stove.

NOTE

Although an expensive stove enhances your S. meals, it is only one of three steps in the cooking process. To maximize the potential of your stove, you need an excellent refrigerator for storage, and a food processor for efficient preparation.

Wild Bill THX-451 Barbecue

Cost: §350

Motive: Hunger (4)

Notes: Only experienced adult chefs should fire up the barbe. Be careful not to position the grill near flammable items.

8R Food Processor

Cost: §220

Motive: Hunger (2)

...es: A food processor speeds up meal preparation and ...ances food quality.

...k Genie Trash Compactor

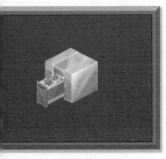

Cost: §375

Motive: None

...es: A compactor holds more garbage than a trash can, and ...n when it is full, it will not degrade the Room rating because ... trash is concealed.

Dish Duster Deluxe

Cost: §550

Motive: Dirty dishes lower your Room score.

Notes: Kids can't use the dishwasher, but it still cuts cleanup time considerably, and the countertop can be used for placing other items (sorry, no eating allowed).

Fuzzy Logic Dishwasher

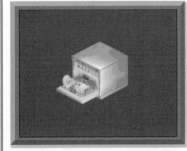

Cost: §950

Motive: Dirty dishes lower your Room score.

Notes: The Cadillac of dishwashers cleans up kitchen messes in a snap. This model has fewer breakdowns than the Dish Duster.

Llamark Refrigerator

Cost: §600

Motive: Hunger (6)

Notes: This model is sufficient while your Sims are building up their Cooking Skills.

Porcina Refrigerator Model P1g-S

Cost: §1,200

Motive: Hunger (7)

Notes: This model produces more satisfying food for your Sims.

Freeze Secret Refrigerator

Cost: §2,500

Motive: Hunger (8)

Notes: The best place to store your food. When it's matched with a food processor, gas stove, and an experienced chef, your Sims will be licking their lips.

Plumbing

Sims can't carry buckets to the well for their weekly bath, and the outhouse hasn't worked in years, so install various plumbing objects to maintain a clean, healthy environment. Of course, not every plumbing object is essential, but you can't beat a relaxing hour in the hot tub with a few of your closest friends (or casual acquaintances).

Hydronomic Kitchen Sink

Cost: §250

Motive: Hygiene (2)

Notes: Without it the Sims would be washing dishes in the bathro

Epikouros Kitchen Sink

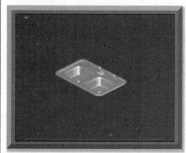

Cost: §500

Motive: Hygiene (3)

Notes: It's twice as big as the single, but a dishwasher is a better investment.

"Andersonville" Pedestal Sink

Cost: §400

Motive: Hygiene (2)

Notes: Neat Sims like to wash their hands after using the toil

eia-O-Matic Toilet

Cost: §300

Motive: Bladder (8)

s: Hey, your only other option is the floor.

h Force 5 XLT

Cost: §1,200

Motives: Comfort (4),
Bladder (8)

s: Your Sims can't go to the ballpark to get a good seat, but
can sit in a lap of luxury in the bathroom.

SpaceMiser Shower

Cost: §650

Motive: Hygiene (6)

Notes: This is basic equipment in a Sims bathroom. One Sim can
shower at a time, and the neat ones tend to linger longer than
the sloppy ones. Sims are generally shy if they are not in love
with a housemate, so you may need more than one shower (and
bathroom) to prevent a traffic jam in the bathroom.

Justa Bathtub

Cost: §800

Motives: Comfort (3),
Hygiene (6)

Notes: Your Sims get a double benefit from a relaxing bath
when they have a little extra time.

Sani-Queen Bathtub

Cost: §1,500

Motives: Comfort (5), Hygiene (8)

Notes: Almost twice the price, but the added Comfort and Hygiene points are worth it.

Hydrothera Bathtub

Cost: §3,200

Motives: Comfort (8), Hygiene (10)

Notes: The most fun a Sim can have alone. Save your Simoleans, buy it, and listen to sounds of relaxation.

WhirlWizard Hot Tub

Cost: §6,500

Motives: Comfort (6), Hygiene (2), Fun (2)

Notes: Up to four adult Sims can relax, mingle, and begin lasting relationships in the hot tub.

Lighting

Sims love natural light, so make sure the sun shi through your windows from every direction. An when the sun goes down, your Sims need plent lighting on the walls, floors, and tables to illuminate their world until bedtime. Although only three lamps listed below have direct impac on the Room score, all of the lamps have a collective effect when spread evenly throughou the home. Pay special attention to key activity areas in the kitchen, family room, bedrooms, ar of course, the bathroom.

CAUTION

Lamp bulbs burn out with use, and they mus be replaced. Sims can replace their own bulb but without Mechanical Skills, they run the risk of electrocution. Hiring a repairman is another option, but at §50 per hour, this can be very costly.

Table Lamps

Bottle Lamp

Cost: §25

Motive: None

n' Haight Lava Lamp

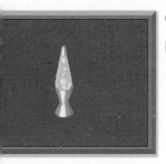

Cost: §80

Motive: Room (2)

SC Electric Co. Antique Lamp

Cost: §300

Motive: Room (1)

miche Table Lamp

Cost: §85

Motive: None

Floor Lamps

Halogen Heaven Lamp by Contempto

Cost: §50

Motive: None

Reflections Chrome Lamp

Cost: §180

Motive: None

Lumpen Lumeniat Floor Lamp

Cost: §100

Motive: None

Torchosteronne Floor Lamp

Cost: §350

Motive: Room (1)

Top Brass Sconce

Cost: §110

Motive: None

Wall Lamps

White Globe Sconce

Cost: §35

Motive: None

Blue Plate Special Sconce

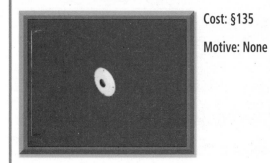

Cost: §135

Motive: None

Oval Glass Sconce

Cost: §85

Motive: None

Outside Lamp

Garden Lamp (Outdoor Use Only)

Cost: §50

Motive: None

scellaneous

re down to the objects that are hard to fit
a category—everything from bookcases to
erage bars. Don't make the mistake of
oring these items because you think they're
uries; your Sim's life would be extremely
icult without a trash can, alarm clock, and
kcase. Plus, if you want to improve your Sim's
risma and Body ratings, you'll need a mirror
exercise machine. So, once you install the
c objects in your house, look to the
cellaneous category for objects that take your
s lifestyle to the next level.

ozMore Alarm Clock

Cost: §30

Motive: None

s: After you set the clock, it will ring two hours before the
ool arrives for every working Sim in your house.

h Can

Cost: §30

Motive: None

s: Without a place to put trash, your Sim house will become
infested hovel.

Magical Mystery Toy Box

Cost: §50

Motive: Fun (2)

Notes: A good entertainment alternative if your kids are getting
bleary-eyed in front of the computer.

Narcisco Wall Mirror

Cost: §100

Motive: Improves
Charisma

Notes: Adults can Practice speech in front of the mirror to
improve their Charisma.

Medicine Cabinet

Cost: §125

Motive: Hygiene (1),
Improves Charisma

Notes: Your Sims can Practice speech in the bathroom and
improve their Hygiene at the same time.

Narcisco Floor Mirror

Cost: §150

Motive: Improves Charisma

Notes: Place this mirror anywhere to practice Charisma without locking other Sims out of the bathroom.

Will Lloyd Wright Doll House

Cost: §180

Motive: Fun (2)

Notes: An engaging group activity for kids and adults.

Cheap Pine Bookcase

Cost: §250

Motive: Fun (1), Improve Cooking, Mechanical, and Study Skills

Notes: Reading books is the best way to prevent premature death from fires or electrocution.

"Dimanche" Folding Easel

Cost: §250

Motive: Fun (2), Impro Creativity

Notes: With practice, a Sim can improve Creativity, and eventually sell a picture for up to §166.

Pinegulcher Dresser

Cost: §250

Motive: None

Notes: A Sim can change into various formal, work, and leisu outfits, and even acquire a new body type.

Kinderstuff Dresser

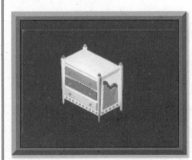

Cost: §300

Motive: None

Notes: Kids like to dress up too!

shim Bookcase

Cost: §500

Motive: Fun (2), Improves Cooking, Mechanical, and Study Skills

s: This expensive bookcase awards Skill points at the same as the cheaper one.

k Matewell Chess Set

Cost: §500

Motive: Fun (2), Improves Logic

s: Serious Sims gain the most Fun points by playing, and two Sims can improve Logic by playing each other.

litional Oak Armoire

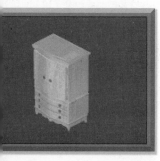

Cost: §550

Motive: Room (1)

: This dresser allows your Sim to change clothes (body). The choices vary, depending upon the Sim's current outfit.

SuperDoop Basketball Hoop

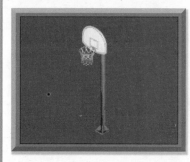

Cost: §650

Motive: Fun (4)

Notes: Active Sims love to play hoops, and any visitor is welcome to join the fun. A Sim with higher Body points performs better on the court.

"Exerto" Benchpress Exercise Machine

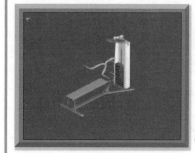

Cost: §700

Motive: Improves Body

Notes: Adult Sims can bulk up their Body points with exercise sessions.

Bachman Wood Beverage Bar

Cost: §800

Motive: Hunger (1), Fun (3), Room (2)

Notes: Every drink lowers the Bladder score, but adult Sims like to make drinks for themselves and friends. Kids can grab a soda from the fridge.

Libri di Regina Bookcase

Cost: §900

Motive: Fun (3), Improves Cooking, Mechanical, and Study Skills

Notes: This stylish bookcase is perfect for a swanky Sim pad, but it still imparts Skill points at the same rate as the pine model.

Antique Armoire

Cost: §1,200

Motive: Room (2)

Notes: A more expensive version of the cheaper armoire, but it adds twice as many Room points.

The Funinator Deluxe

Cost: §1,200

Motive: Fun (5)

Notes: When the house is swarming with kids, send them outside to raise their Fun bar and burn some energy.

Chimeway & Daughters Piano

Cost: §3,500

Motive: Fun (4), Room Improves Creativity

Notes: The most creative Sims will produce more beautiful music. The better the music, the greater the chance that listeners will like it. If a listener does not like the music, both Sims' Relationship scores will deteriorate.

Aristoscratch Pool Table

Cost: §4,200

Motive: Fun (6)

Notes: Up to two Sims use the table at the same time. Make sure that you allow enough room for Sims to get to the table and walk around it during play.

CHAPTER 7: ALL IN THE FAMILY

Introduction

Up to this point, we've covered the mechanics of *The Sims*. By now you should be familiar with creating families, building houses, buying objects, and getting jobs; and you should have considerable insight into how a Sim thinks and acts. Now, let's put it all together and join several Sim households in action. In this chapter we introduce you to working Sims families, ranging from one-Sim homes to larger households with kids and babies. Finally, we take an in-depth look at one of the toughest challenges in *The Sims*: building positive (and long-lasting) Relationships.

You Can Make It Alone

The biggest difficulty in being a bachelor is that you have to do everything yourself (sounds like real life, doesn't it?). You'll need to cook, clean, and improve your Skills, while at the same time keep up with a work schedule and satisfy your personal Motives. There's always time for Fun, and a good sofa or easy chair will provide a measure of Comfort. However, it's impossible to socialize while at work, and you will be frustrated watching neighbors drop by during the day and then leave when no one answers the door.

The Single Sim's Career

As a lone Sim you must choose a job that has decent hours and light friendship demands. This leaves a Military career as your only option. At most levels you work a six-hour day, and you won't need a single friend for the first five levels. A promotion to Level 6 requires one friend, but that can be established after you refine your schedule.

Designing a Bachelor Pad

There are several considerations when designing and furnishing a house for one Sim. Review the following checklist before you place your first wall stake.

Fig. 7-1. It's ha the lap of luxu but you have everything yo need to get a keep your san and learn how to cook.

- **Keep your house small, and place the front door close to the street. This allows you to milk a few extra minutes out of every morning before meeting the car pool.**
- **The interior should include a bedroom, bathroom, and living room. Rather than add family room, use an outside patio area for Fu objects and an exercise machine. A Military career requires an ever-increasing number of Body Skill points.**
- **Install only enough counter space to place a food processor and prepare your meals. This leaves more space for a table and chairs. Buy at least two chairs so that you can socialize with a friend while sharing a meal.**
- **Without the space or the budget to buy expensive sofas or recliners, get a top-of-the-line bed, which enables your Sim to get by o fewer hours of sleep. Buy an inexpensive nightstand for an alarm clock, and add a few wall lights to boost your Room score.**
- **You'll need a computer for your job search, but keep in mind that you can return it withi 24 Sim-hours for a full refund. Find your Military job and then pack up the PC.**

y an expensive refrigerator to maximize
e quality of your food, but don't bother
th a stove until your Sim learns how
cook.

cause of your career, there's no need to
cialize until you are up for promotion to
vel 6, so don't waste money on living room
airs or an expensive sofa. A cheap TV will
ovide enough Fun for now.

aving the Single Life

ntually you will tire of the solitary lifestyle,
ch, thanks to the romantic tendencies of most
, is not a problem. The first step is friendship.
r the Relationship bar tops 70, your Sim needs
ay on the romance, with plenty of kissing and
ging. Eventually, the Propose option will
ear on the menu.

Fig. 7-2. The kissin' and huggin' pays off; now it's time to pop the question.

A marriage proposal can only take place in the
e of the proposer, so set the mood (you know,
ty your Bladder somewhere other than on the floor,
n up yesterday's dishes, and hide those overdue
. After accepting the proposal, your new spouse
es into your place, along with a good job (a good
g) and plenty of money (a really good thing). But,
osing does not guarantee a positive response. For
mple, a Sim will never accept the proposal on an
ty stomach, so you might want to eat dinner first.

Fig. 7-3. "We're alone, the time is perfect, and I've got grass stains on my knee."

Fig. 7-4. "Nope, sorry, I can't marry you on an empty stomach. Besides, your current lover is hiding in the bushes."

Keep in mind that you have to create potential
mates, because the game won't provide them. You
might as well choose compatible personalities, and
it doesn't hurt to spend some time on career
development. Remember that another Sim can
also propose to you in his or her house; so unless
you want to change residences, hold the romantic
interludes at your place.

NOTE

After marriage, your Sim will still share a bed
with any other Sim with a high enough
Friendship score (over 70), so don't be surprised
if your Sim ends up on the couch when his
buddy beats him to the sack.

Fig. 7-5. When two Sims decide to get married, they change clothes and complete the ceremony within seconds.

Interestingly, if your future spouse already has children, and at least one adult still resides in his or her original house, the kids stay. So, your new spouse arrives with job and bank account intact, sans kids. What a deal!

That isn't the only unusual aspect of married life in SimsVille. Marriage is not sacred here, at least not in the legal sense. A Sim can have multiple mates all living under the same roof, as pictured in figure 7-6. The interpersonal dynamics can sometimes get a little dicey, but it's workable, and the extra income is great!

Fig. 7-6. After the wedding, our Sim bride goes to bed with her former boyfriend.

TIP

A three-way relationship makes it easier to have babies. Not only are there additional combinations for procreation, but you can also have one of the working adults take a night job, so there is a caregiver for the baby during the day. Even with staggered schedules, there will be at least one sleepless Sim until the baby matures, so don't get too complacent with this arrangement.

Married, with Children

After your Sims promise undying love and devotion to each other (or, at least until the next promotion), it's time to have a baby. Actually, your Sims can live together for years without having children, but if they do, you'll be missing one of the The Sims' most vexing experiences.

Conception

The exercise of making a baby is similar to the steps taken to activate the marriage Proposal option. First, get a male and female Sim together and then concentrate on strengthening their relationship. When both Sims are obviously enjoying each other's company, lay on the hugs and kisses. Keep smooching until you receive the option to have a baby, as pictured in figure 7-7.

Fig. 7-7. A little bundle of joy is a click away.

f you answer yes, a bassinet appears almost antly, amid an explosion of dandelions. The py couple celebrates the new arrival, then they kly go back to their daily routine. This baby g is a snap. Well, not exactly.

Fig. 7-8. Yippee! It's a boy!

n short order, the little bundle of joy starts aming. A Sim will eventually respond to the s, but rather than wait, get someone to the y immediately. Clicking on the bassinet reveals ee options: Feed, Play, or Sing. When in doubt, d the baby, but be prepared to come right k with Play or Sing when the baby starts ling again.

Fig. 7-9. Kids do a great job entertaining the baby during one of its frequent crying sessions.

This mayhem continues for three Sim days, during which time the household will be in an uproar. Forget about getting eight hours of beauty sleep. Designate one Sim as primary caregiver, preferably one who does not work, because the baby's cries wake any Sim in the room. The first day is nonstop crying. By the second day, the baby sleeps for a few hours at a time; take advantage of the break and send the caregiver to bed. As long as you stay responsive, the baby evolves into a runny-nosed kid, and the family can get back to normal. However, if you spend too much time in the hot tub and not enough time with the baby, a social service worker will march into your house and take the baby, as pictured in figure 7-10. You'll only receive one warning, so don't take this responsibility lightly.

Fig. 7-10. We hardly knew the little tyke!

NOTE

The bassinet appears near the spot where your Sims made the decision to have a baby. Although the Sims cannot move the bassinet, you can use the Hand Tool to move it. Pick a location that is isolated from other sleeping areas, so the disturbance is kept to a minimum.

Building and Maintaining Healthy Relationships

Gathering an ever-increasing number of friends is critical for career advancement, especially at the higher levels. It is also your Sims' only way to build up their Social scores and fend off frequent bouts of depression. In this section we outline the steps required for finding potential friends, building up positive feelings, and then maintaining healthy relationships.

Talk Is Cheap

The easiest way to make friends is often overlooked, because it is uneventful compared to other social events. However, you can almost always initiate a conversation between Sims (regardless of their Friendship scores), and keep it going for a very long time. During this benign exchange of thought balloons, you can usually nudge the Friendship score in a positive direction. When starting from 0 it takes a few encounters to get over 50 (true friendship), but once you reach this threshold, the action picks up considerably. Our newly married Sims went from a score of 64 to a marriage proposal in one evening. Although the woman eventually declined because her stomach was growling, she proposed the next day and the marriage was consummated.

Fig. 7-11. Keep talking and your Friendship score will grow.

Finding Time to Socialize

After your Sim starts working, it's difficult to fir time to call other Sims and arrange meetings. Mornings are worst, although you have more options if your neighborhood has several non-working Sims. Your best bet is to start socializin right after coming home from work. Take care personal needs first—Hygiene and Bladder—an then "Serve Dinner." Don't let a bad chef get n the stove; you can't afford to waste time puttin out a fire or your guests will leave. With a coun full of food, your friends head straight for the kitchen, where you can chat over a plate of Sim grub and then plan the rest of your evening.

Positive Social Events

After everyone is finished eating, take a little ti for pleasant conversation. In the case of the female Sims pictured in figure 7-11, there is a lo of fence mending to accomplish, because one ju stole the other's love interest. But, Sims are generally forgiving, and a quarrel can be mende with a few drinks, a game of pool, or a long soa in the hot tub.

Ideally, your house has an entertainment roor with group activity items such as a pool table, stereo, or beverage bar. After you get everyone i the room, keep them busy with a string of activit Even our former lovers can't resist a dance when the music starts playing, as pictured in figure 7-12

Fig. 7-12. Our S guy is enjoying dance with his former girlfrien although his cu wife will proba slap him when music stops playing (if she can stay awake long enough).

CAUTION

...oid close activities such as dancing, hugging, ...c. when the current spouse or love interest is ...the room. When the dance was over (figure ...12), our Sim wife did indeed slap her new ...sband, causing her recently mended ...lationship score with the other woman to ...op from +14 to −7.

...One of the most difficult aspects of ...ertaining in the evening is keeping the host ...m falling asleep on the floor. After a hard day's ...rk, most Sims begin nodding out around 10:00 ...1. You can squeeze a little extra time out of the ...ning if they take a short nap after coming ...me from work. Be prepared for a grouchy Sim ...he morning (figure 7-13) if the evening's ...ivities stretch too far into the night.

Fig. 7-13. Our tired party girl hurries off to the car pool without a shower— not a good way to impress her superiors.

...ter your guests arrive, you need to ...icromanage your Sims so they don't go off ...d take care of their own needs. Obviously, ...u must pay attention to a full Bladder, but ...u can delay other actions by redirecting your ...ms to group activities. Break up the party ...hen your Sims are teetering on the edge of ...xhaustion or they'll fall asleep on the floor.

CAUTION

Visiting Sims generally hang around until 1:00 a.m. or later, which is undoubtedly past your bedtime. Direct your Sims to bed at the appropriate time, or they may feel compelled to hang out with their guests until well past midnight, as pictured in figure 7-14.

Fig. 7-14. Our host Sim is still cleaning up dishes when he should be asleep.

Stockpiling Potential Friends

When your career advances to the top promotion level, you need more than 10 friends in every career except the Military. Hence, it's a good idea to create a few additional families early in the game, and you might want to fill one house with the maximum of eight Sims to dramatically increase your pool.

Visitors Coming and Going

The following tables include important information on how and why visitors do the things they do. You may not be able to directly control your guests' actions, but at least you won't take it personally when they decide to split.

Visitors' Starting Motives

MOTIVE	STARTING VALUE
Bladder	0 to 30
Comfort	30 to 70
Energy	35
Fun	-20 to 20
Hunger	-30 to -20
Hygiene	90
Social	-50 to -40

In a perfect Sim-world, visitors leave your house just past 1:00 a.m. However if one of their Motives falls into the danger zone, they will depart earlier. When this happens, the Sim's thought balloon reveals a reason for the early exit.

Visitors' Leaving Motives

MOTIVE	DROPS BELOW THIS VALUE
Bladder	-90
Comfort	-70
Energy	-80
Fun	-55
Hunger	-50
Hygiene	-70
Mood	-75
Room	-100
Social	-85

Guest Activities

There are three types of visitor activities: those initiated by a family member, shared activities, and autonomous activities where guests are on their own. The following sections and tables describe each type.

Activities Initiated by Family Member

One of the Sims under your control must prepare food or turn on the TV before visitors can join in. Turning on the TV takes a second, but you need little prep time for a meal. It's a good idea to begin meal preparation immediately after inviting friends over.

Shared Activities

A Sim can start any of the following activities and then invite the participation of a guest.

OBJECT	VISITORS' INVOLVEMENT
Basketball Hoop	Join
Chess	Join
Dollhouse	Watch
Hot Tub	Join
Pinball Machine	Join
Play Structure	Join
Piano	Watch
Pool Table	Join
Stereo	Join, Dance
Train Set	Watch

onomous Activities

ting Sims can begin any of the following vities on their own.

itors' Autonomous Activities

JECT	AUTONOMOUS ACTION
quarium	Watch Fish
aby	Play
ar	Have a Drink
hair	Sit
hair (Recliner)	Sit
offee (Espresso Machine)	Drink Espresso
offeemaker	Drink Coffee
re	Panic
amingo	View
ountain	Play
ava Lamp	View
ainting	View
ool	Swim
ool Diving Board	Dive In
ool Ladder	Get In/Out
culpture	View
ink	Wash Hands
ofa	Sit
oilet	Use, Flush
ombstone/Urn	Mourn
oy Box	Play
rash Can (Inside)	Dispose

cial Interactions

e results of various interactions are best learned experience because of the individual personality its that come into play. However, it helps to ve an idea what each action may produce. The lowing table offers notes on each interaction.

INTERACTION	DESCRIPTION
Back Rub	When well-received, it is a good transition into kissing and hugging, but the Relationship score should already be over 50.
Brag	This is what mean Sims do to your Sim. Don't use it, unless you want to ruin a good friendship.
Compliment	Generally positive, but you should withhold compliments until your Relationship score is above 15.
Dance	Great activity between friends (40+), but it almost always causes a jealous reaction from a jilted lover.
Entertain	A somewhat goofy activity, but it usually works well with other Playful Sims.
Fight	Don't do it (unless you know you can take the other Sim!).
Flirt	A great way to boost a strong Relationship (70+) into the serious zone, but watch your back. Flirting usually triggers a jealous reaction from significant others.
Give Gift	A benign way to say you like the other Sim, or that you're sorry for acting like an idiot at the last party; best used with 40+ Relationship scores.
Hug	This one's always fun if the hug-ee's Relationship score is +60; a good transition to kisses, and then a marriage proposal.
Joke	Good between casual friends (+15) who are both Playful.
Kiss	The relationship is heating up, but if a jealous ex or current lover is in the vicinity, someone could get slapped.
Talk	The starting point of every friendship.
Tease	Why bother, unless you don't like the other Sim.
Tickle	Not as positive as it might seem, but Playful Sims are definitely more receptive.

CHAPTER 8:
A DAY IN THE LIFE

Introduction

[No]w, it's time to turn on our Sim-Cam and follow [fe]w of our families as they handle the ups and [dow]ns of Sim life. In this chapter we switch to a [scra]pbook format, with screenshots of our Sims [in] interesting—and sometimes compromising— [situ]ations. Admittedly, we coaxed our Sims into [som]e of these dilemmas. But it's all in fun, and we [thin]k it's the best way for you to get a feel for this [ama]zing game.

As the Sim Turns

Our third adult roommate, Mortimer, just returned home from his night shift, so for now, his needs are secondary. We put him to work mopping the kitchen floor (the dishwasher broke last night, but everyone was falling asleep, so we figured it would keep until morning).

Five o'clock wake-up call is not pretty. Even with full Energy bars, your Sims can be a little cranky, but don't give them any slack. Get the best chef into the kitchen pronto, to serve breakfast for everyone in the house.

Before we are accused of being sexist, we should explain that the only reason Bella is cooking for everyone is that she is the most experienced chef. If Mark turns on the stove, chances are the kitchen will burn down. We promise to boost his Cooking Skills at the first opportunity.

Switching to Zoomed Out view is a good way to manage the household early in the morning. This way you can quickly target important tasks for completion before the car pool arrives.

Mark is, well, busy at the moment. It's too bad he doesn't gain Energy points for sitting on the toilet, because he stayed up much too late last night. A good breakfast helps, but getting through the day won't be easy, and he can forget about any promotions thanks to his sub-par mood.

Prima's Official Strategy Guide

It's a nice family breakfast with husband Mortimer on the left, wife Bella on the right, and Bella's ex-boyfriend Mark in the middle. However, there isn't much time for chitchat, because the car pool has arrived, and it will leave at a few minutes past nine.

After cancelin[g] thoughts abo[ut] sleeping, we [...] on Mark's car[...] pool. He chan[ges] clothes faster [than] Superman an[d] sprints to his [...] in the nick of time. Have a [good] day, Mark!

Bella is on her way to the car pool and we have about a half hour to get Mark in gear, which may be a problem due to his low Energy rating. Unfortunately, Bella's Hygiene leaves much to be desired. We make a mental note to get her into the shower before bedtime tonight so she'll be fresh as a daisy in the morning).

Poor Mortimer[...] We've been so [...] focused on get[ting] Bella and Mark [to] work, we didn'[t] notice that the [...] slob is asleep [on his] feet! We need [to] wake him up ([he'll] be so happy), a[nd] send him to be[d.]

Uh-oh, big time problem with Mark. He's standing in the kitchen in his pajamas, in a catatonic state. With only a half hour to get to the car pool, we need to shake him up a little and point him to the door.

We receive a reminder that Mortimer's car [pool] arrives at 4:00 [...] Unfortunately w[e] forgot to set his alarm, and his Hygiene and Bladder bars ha[ve] gone south, so w[e] need to wake hi[m] up soon. Fortunately, he a[te] before bedtime, so he can probably get by without a big meal.

Mortimer is up and he's not happy. With the amount of time remaining before his car pool shows up, he can empty his bladder and get in half a shower before racing out the door.

Mark is well rested, so he can fend for himself this morning. He steps into the shower as the car pool arrives, so he has almost one hour to get ready. But, while in the shower, he decides to take the day off and join Bella.

With Mortimer out of the house, we can concentrate on Bella and Mark, who have both arrived home from work. Mark socialized a little too much the night before, so he went straight to bed without any prompting.

The three housemates share a pleasant breakfast together. Perhaps they have finally buried the hatchet after the Mortimer-Bella-Mark thing. We can only hope.

Mortimer arrives home at 1:00 a.m.. After a bathroom break and quick shower, we send him straight to bed so he can party with Bella tomorrow, who has decided to take the day off.

Mark grabs the phone to invite a friend over, but before he can dial, a local radio station calls with great news. He just won §550 in a promotion!

Mark calls a friend, who says he'll be right over. While Mark changes into his Speedo, Mortimer, Jeff, and Bella enjoy a dip in the pool. That's right, Mortimer missed his car pool, too. It's a day off (without pay) for the entire house!

After dinner, Jeff heads for home. Bella and Mark retreat to the de where Bella rubs Mark's back.

It's on to the hot tub for a long, relaxing soak. Comfort, Hygiene, Social, and Fun scores are soaring. It's too bad we have to eat and empty our Bladders or we'd never leave!

One good rub deserves a hug, things suddenly heat up betweer the former lover

Everyone will be hungry after the swim and soak, so Bella hops out to make dinner. Soon, everyone grabs a plate and starts discussing what life will be like when they are all unemployed. Everyone, that is, except Mortimer, who prefers standing.

Mortimer takes look at the lip-locked Sims and heads straight f the bar.

After a couple of adult beverages, Mortimer follows the lovers into the hallway where they are still groping each other like teenagers on prom night.

Bella drives off to work while our two Sim-Neanderthals take their fight to the bathroom.

Mortimer shows his frustration by slapping Mark across the cheek (he's such an animal). Bella is disgusted and goes upstairs to bed.

What will become of our star-crossed lovers?

Will Bella leave Mortimer and go back to Mark?

Will Mark feel guilty about wrecking Mortimer's marriage, and move in with the Newbies?

Will Bella reveal what she and Jeff were really doing in the hot tub?

Who will clean up the bathroom?

For the answers to these burning questions, stay tuned for the next episode of...*As the Sim Turns*.

Life with the Pleasants

One slap turns to another and seven hours later, Mortimer and Mark are still duking it out.

Jeff experiences the joys of working a night shift—cleaning up his family's dinner dishes...

...and taking out the trash at four in the morning.

Skeeter misses too many days school and ge bad news—he his way to mil school, never seen again.

Everyone is asleep, so Jeff takes an opportunity to practice his Charisma in front of the bathroom mirror. Unfortunately for Jeff, the walking dead also take this opportunity to float through the mirror and scare the •&$%$# out of him.

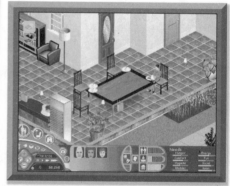

Although his ic has already disappeared fr the control par Skeeter enjoys last breakfast before he is ex from the game

Like all kids, Daniel and Skeeter can only make snacks on their own, so someone must serve their breakfast before school.

Not wanting to follow in his brother's foots Daniel hits the books and imp his grades.

Hmmm. Which pile should I pay first, the red one or the yellow one? Get a clue, Jeff—if you don't pay the red ones, they'll repossess your furniture!

Pity the Poor Bachelor

With garbage a foot thick on the floor of his house, our bachelor decides to stay outside and entertain a new lady friend with his juggling act.

The Maid should get riot pay for all the garbage this family leaves on the floor!

"Wow, she really likes me! Maybe she won't notice the garbage if I invite her inside."

Maids are limited to cleaning up Sim-messes, but that frees up the family to take care of other important needs, like advancing their skills. Diane Pleasant takes a break to bone up on her Mechanical Skills. Perhaps she

"I really like you Bella, so I got you a pair of basketball shoes!"

fix the dishwasher and save §50-an-hour repair bills.

Bachelors on a fixed budget can have a difficult time having fun. A basketball hoop in the back yard is a good investment, and if you can find a Playful friend, it's a cheap date, too.

"Excuse me, so could you pleas move out of th fire so I can extinguish it?"

Kids Are People, Too

Armed with a new gas stove and absolutely no cooking ability, this bachelor decides to flame-broil the kitchen.

Toy boxes are s and relatively inexpensive. If are placed in th bedroom, your kids can sneak little Fun time before school.

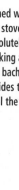

Whew, the fireman is here to put out the fire. There's only one problem: he can't get into the house because our hero is standing in front of the stove, which happens to be next to the door. We understand that the bachelor's quarters are tight, but it's probably not a good idea to put the stove next to the front door. By the time the fireman makes his way to the back door, your bachelor could be toast.

Children have fe inhibitions, but still don't like t use the bathroo front of the Mai their siblings.

Skeeter and Matthew enjoy a little Social and Fun time playing with their railroad town.

Left to their own devices, kids often stay up long past the time their parents hit the sack. In fact, even with Free Will activated, parents feel no responsibility for getting their children to bed early. So, if you forget to send the kids to bed, get ready for some serious tantrums in the morning.

Skillful Sims

An exercise machine is the obvious choice for improving a Sim's Body Skill, but if you can keep your Sims in the pool, they'll increase Body scores even faster, and boost Fun at the same time.

Unlike the railroad, the pinball machine is a solo activity.

Unlike adults, who need toys for their playtime, kids can play with each other.

Sometimes it can be hard to get your Sims to slow down long enough for serious Skill enhancement, especially if it means sitting down to read. The solution is simple: Place two comfortable chairs close to the bookcase, and give each Sim different Skill assignments. Remember that you only need one Cooking expert and one Mechanical expert in the same house. Divide reading assignments appropriately to bring their Skills quickly up to speed.

You might be concerned about an adult male who stands for hours in front of a full-length mirror in his Speedo. However, it makes sense to place a mirror in the family room for easier access. This way, your Sims won't tie up the bathroom practicing Charisma in the mirror over the sink.

Increasing the Creativity Skill through painting has an added bonus—the ability to sell your painting. But, don't get too excited; a bad painting fetches only §1 on the open market.

With minimal Mechanical Skill, repairing this shower seems to take forever, and all the while, Mark's Comfort and Energy scores are dropping. Maybe a Repairman is worth the price until Mark earns a few more Mechanical points.

As the Sim Turns: Part Two

As we return to Sim soap, Mortim has just returned from another nig shift, and after a light snack, he decides to take early morning sw thinking that Ma and Bella are bu getting ready fo work. After swimming a few laps, he is ready to go to bed, but wait...where is the ladder? "I can't get out of the pool!" says Mortimer, frantically. "I'll just tread water for a while until Mark or Bella come out. If I can just...keep... going...getting tired... so tired...."

Mark and Bella finally come outside, but it's late. Poor Mortir exhausted and confused, has already dropped like a stone to t bottom of the p

After Mortimer's body is removed from the pool, a tombstone is erected on the s where the ladde used to be. If Mortimer were s here, he would h appreciated the humor...maybe

After getting over the initial shock, Mark and Bella grieve at the site where their "friend" died.

"O.K., enough grieving," says Bella, as she tells Mark a real knee-slapper.

After some welcome comic relief, the two mourners console each other with a supportive hug. Right.

Then, they console each other further...with a dance?

Thinking the time is right (and that they have carried on the charade long enough), Mark pulls Bella close for a kiss. But, much to Mark's surprise, Bella suddenly cools and pushes him away.

What is this strange turn of events?

Did Bella entice Mark into helping her solve the "Mortimer" problem, only to leave him in the lurch?

Find the answers on the next episode of *As the Sim Turns*, on a computer near you!

Sims in the Kitchen

In the Motives chapter, we provided a basic explanation of how Sims satisfy their Hunger score. As you know by now, food is readily available in the refrigerator, 24 hours a Sim-day. The supply is endless, and you never have to go to the market. However, the difference between what is in the refrigerator and what a Sim actually eats lies in the preparation. The following screens take you through the various options available to a Sim chef, and the table at the end of this chapter explains how the different appliances and countertops modify the quality of each meal.

After processir food, Bella thro it in a pot and works her mag Two more mod are at work he Bella's Cooking Skill and the special feature of the Pyrotorr Gas Range.

The snack, a §5 bag of chips, is the lowest item on the Sim food chain. It's better than nothing when your Sim is racing around getting ready for the car pool, but it barely nudges the Hunger bar.

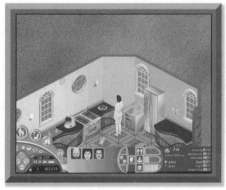

When the meal finished, Bella places a stack of plates on the counter.

For a much more satisfying meal, direct the best chef in the house to Prepare a Meal. In this screen, Bella is getting ready to throw the raw ingredients into the food processor (a positive modifier, as noted in the table). While one Sim prepares breakfast, you can assign the other Sims to menial labor, such as mopping or picking up garbage.

Thrilled that he doesn't have to his own tastele slop, Mark gra a plate from the counter.

Another option for preparing multiple portions is to call out for a pizza. This is a good choice for a Sim who has a low Cooking Skill. Rather than using the stove and setting the kitchen on fire, a telephone and §40 will buy a hot pie, delivered to the door in an hour.

The Sims love their pizza, and they can't wait to set it down and grab a slice. So, don't be surprised if your Sim plops the carton down on the first available counter—even in the bathroom—and starts grazing.

How Appliances and Surfaces Affect Hunger Score

APPLIANCE/SURFACE	HUNGER POINTS ADDED TO MEAL
Dishwasher	5
Trash Compactor	5
Fridge (Llamark)	9
Toaster Oven	9 (plus Cooking Skill)
Fridge (Porcina)	12
Counter (Barcelona)	16
Counter (NuMica)	16
Counter (Tiled)	16
Fridge (Freeze Secret)	16
Microwave	16 (plus Cooking Skill)
Food Processor	32
Stove (Dialectric)	32 (plus 1.5 x Cooking Skill)
Stove (Pyrotorre)	48 (plus 1.5 x Cooking Skill)

CHAPTER 9:
SURVIVAL TIPS

ntroduction

beauty of playing *The Sims* is that everyone's
erience is different. When you take a serious
roach to shaping your family, the game can
for your own life. However, if you mismanage
r Sims, they can sink into despair, waving their
e arms in the air over failed relationships, poor
er decisions, or even a bad mattress. You can
ays delete your family and start over. But then
would never get that warm, fuzzy feeling that
es from turning your pitiful Sims' world into
ngri La.

his chapter is devoted to the *Sims* player who
ts to go the distance and fight the good fight.
ause most Sim problems can be traced back to
or more deficient Motive scores, we have
nged the following tips into separate Motive
ions. Although some of the information is
ered in other chapters, this is meant to be a
k-reference guide for times of crisis. Simply
to the appropriate Motive and save your Sim's
with one of our game-tested tips.

Of course, you can also take a more devious
roach to satisfying or altering your Sim's needs.
Cheats section gives you a bundle of unofficial
mands to rock your Sim's world. We take no
onsibility for the results. (In other words, don't
e crying to us if you stick your Sim in a room
no doors and he or she drops dead!).

Hunger

Maximize Food Quality and Preparation Time

For the best food quality, upgrade *all* appliances
and countertops. Anything short of the most
expensive refrigerator, countertop, stove, etc.,
reduces the potential Hunger value of your meals.
Preparing a meal quickly is all about kitchen
design. Align your objects in the order of
preparation, beginning with the refrigerator,
followed by the food processor (figure 9-1), and
then ending with the stove (figure 9-2).

Fig. 9-1. The food goes from the refrigerator directly to the food processor.

Fig. 9-2. Next stop is the stove, right next door.

Have an open countertop next to the stove on the other side so the food preparer can set the plates down (figure 9-3). Although it has nothing to do with preparation, position the kitchen table and chairs close to the stove so that your Sims can grab their food, sit down together, and boost their Social scores (figure 9-4).

Fig. 9-5. After making dinner hard-working can go to bed and sleep late the morning.

Fig. 9-3. From the stove, the chef moves just a couple steps to the counter and sets down the plates.

Fig. 9-4. If your Sims are prompted to eat, they'll be ready to grab a plate as soon as it hits the counter, and with the table nearby, they can eat, chat, and make it to work on time.

Designate one Sim as your chef. Make sure that Sim has easy access to a chair and bookcase, and then set aside time each day to Study Cooking. When the resident chef's Cooking Skill reaches 10, you have achieved the pinnacle of food preparation.

Make Breakfast the Night Before

Sim food lasts for at least seven hours before the flies arrive and the food is officially inedible. If you have one Sim in the house who doesn't work, have him or her prepare breakfast for everyone at around midnight, as pictured in figure 9-5.

After the food is on the counter, immediate send the Sim to bed. Most Sims should get up b or the very latest, 6 a.m. to be on time for their morning jobs (the chef can sleep in). When everyone comes downstairs, breakfast (it's reall dinner, but Sims don't care what you call it, as as it doesn't have flies) will be on the counter (figure 9-6), fresh and ready to go. You'll save a least 20 Sim-minutes of morning prep time.

Fig. 9-6. It's o 5:30 a.m., but Sim kid is alre eating breakf After taking c his Hygiene, h still have time studying or boosting his score before school bus ar

omfort

en You Gotta Go, Go in Style

oilet is often overlooked as a source of
nfort. The basic Hygeia-O-Matic Toilet costs only
0, but it provides zero Comfort. Spend the
a §900 and buy the Flush Force 5 XLT (figure 9-
Your Sims have to use the bathroom anyway, so
y might as well enjoy the +4 Comfort rating
ry time they take a seat.

Fig. 9-7. You can live
with a black-and-
white TV for a
while, but it doesn't
make sense to do
without the added
comfort of the
Flush Force.

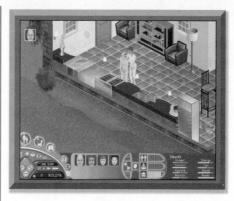

Fig. 9-8. Our Sim is
hungry, but he
always has time
to receive a nice
Back Rub.

Hygiene

Your Mother Was Right

One of the biggest contributors to declining
Hygiene is the lack of hand washing after using
the bathroom (in the Sims and in real life). If your
Sim does not have a Neat personality, you may
need to initiate this action. If you keep it up
throughout the day, your Sim will be in better
shape in the morning, when a shorter shower can
be the difference between making the car pool or
missing a day of work.

b Your Sim the Right Way

ng another Sim a Back Rub is a great way to
ease your chances of seeing Hug, and
ntually Kiss on the social interaction menu.
vever, don't forget that it also raises the
pient's Comfort level. If your Sim's Comfort
l is down, even after a long night's sleep, try a
Back Rubs. It will send your Sim to work in a
er mood, which might be just enough to earn
next promotion.

Fig. 9-9. This Sim
has an average
Neat rating, which
means she won't
always wash her
hands after using
the bathroom. A
few gentle
reminders are
in order.

Flush Your Troubles Away

Sad but true, sloppy Sims don't flush (figure 9-10). It's easy to overlook this nasty habit during a busy day, but it could lead to trouble. A clogged toilet may not affect Hygiene directly, but if your Sim is forced to pee on the floor because the toilet is not working, the Hygiene score drops dramatically.

Fig. 9-10. Second time tonight for this soldier, and we're still waiting for the first flush.

Bladder

Sorry, there's no magic formula for relieving a full Bladder. However, to guard against emergencies and the resulting puddles on the floor, try building two semi-private stalls in your bathroom. This allows two Sims to use the facilities without infringing on each other's privacy, as pictured in figure 9-11.

Fig. 9-11. Dual stalls improve the traffic flow (and other flows) in the bathroom.

Energy

Getting Enough Sleep with Baby

Nothing drains a Sim's Energy bar faster than having a baby in the house (figure 9-12). If you want to survive the three-day baby period with everyone losing their jobs, you must sleep when the baby sleeps. Most likely, this will be in the middle of the day, because Sim babies, like their real counterparts, couldn't care less about their parents' sleep schedules. The baby will not sleep for a full eight hours; however, if you get five or six hours of sleep with the baby, you'll have enough Energy to carry out other important household tasks.

Fig. 9-12. This mom is at the of her rope, and baby is just get warmed up.

Kids Make Great Babysitters

It does nothing for their Fun or Social levels, bu Sim kids will dutifully care for their baby sibling When they come home from school, feed them allow a short play period, and then lock them i the room with the baby (if you're feeling partic ularly sadistic, you can go into Build mode and wall them in). They usually respond on their ow but you can always direct them to the crib, as pictured in figure 9-13, (unless they are too exhausted and need sleep). Take advantage of time by sending the regular caregiver to bed fc some much-needed sleep.

Fig. 9-13. Big brother makes a great nanny.

Favorite Fun Activities

TRAIT	BEST ACTIVITIES
Neat	N/A
Outgoing	TV (Romance), Hot Tub, Pool (if Playful is also high)
Active	Basketball, Stereo (dance), Pool, TV (Action)
Lazy	TV (as long as it's on, they're happy!), Computer, Book
Playful	Any fun object, including Computer, Dollhouse, Train Set, VR Glasses, Pinball, etc. If also Active, shift to Basketball, Dance, and Pool.
Serious	Chess, Newspaper, Book, Paintings (just let them stare)
Nice	Usually up for anything
Mean	TV (Horror)

...un

...ding the Right Activity for Your Sim

...ess your Sims live in a monastery, you should
...e plenty of Fun objects in your house. The trick
...atching the right kind of activity with a Sim's
...sonality. In the frenzy of daily schedules and
...ntaining Relationships, it's easy to lose touch
...h your Sim's personality traits. Visit the
...sonality menu often (click on the "head" icon)
...eview the five traits. Make sure you have at
...t one of the following objects readily available
...our Sim (the bedroom is a good spot).

NOTE

...Sim should have at least six points (bars) in
...e of the following traits to maximize the
...ommended activity. Of course, an even
...her number produces faster Fun rewards. To
...alify for the opposite trait (e.g., Active/Lazy,
...yful/Serious) a Sim should have no more
...an three points in the trait).

When in Doubt, Entertain Someone

If your Sim does not have access to a Fun activity,
simply Entertain someone for an instant Fun (and
Social) boost, as pictured in figure 9-14. You can
usually repeat this activity several times, and it
doesn't take much time (great for kids on busy
school mornings).

Fig. 9-14. When a good toy is not around, Sim kids love to Entertain each other.

Social

Satisfying Social requirements can be very frustrating, especially when Sims are on different work or sleep schedules. Socializing is a group effort, so plan small parties on a regular basis. Keep a notepad with all of your Sims' work schedules, so you know whom to invite at any time of the day.

- It's O.K. to ask your guests to leave. After you shmooze a little and boost your Relationship score, send the Sim packing, and call up a different one. Use this round-robin approach to maintain all of your friendships.

- Don't let Mean Sims abuse you. This can be tough to control if you're not paying attention. When you're socializing with a Mean Sim, keep an eye on the activity queue in the screen's upper-left corner. If that Sim's head pops up (without you initiating it), it probably says "Be Teased by...," or "Be Insulted by...." Simply click on the icon to cancel the negative event and maintain your Relationship score. Once you diffuse the threat, engage the Sim in simple talking, or move your Sim into a group activity (pool table, hot tub, pool, etc.)

- Unless you like being the bad guy, don't advertise your advances toward one Sim if you already have a Relationship with another. Sims are extremely jealous, but you can still maintain multiple love Relationships as long as you don't flaunt them in public.

Room

A Room score crisis is easy to remedy. If you have the money, simply add more lights and painting Also check the quality of objects in the room, a upgrade whenever possible. If your room is jammed with expensive objects, lights, and paintings and your Room score is still low, there must be a mess somewhere. A normally maxed Room score can slip with so much as a puddle o the floor (as pictured in figure 9-15). Clean up t mess to restore the Room score to its normal lev

Fig. 9-15. It lo like someone short of the to A mop will tak care of the me and raise the Room score.

Scan your house on a regular basis for the following negative Room factors:

- Dead plants
- Cheap objects (especially furniture)
- Puddles (they can also indicate a bad appliance; when in doubt, click on the item to see if Repair comes up as an option)
- Dark areas
- If you have the money, replace items taken b the Repo guy.

heats

tivate the cheat command line at any time during
game by pressing Ctrl + Shift + C. An input box
pears in the screen's upper left corner. Type in one
the codes listed below. You must re-activate the
mmand line after each cheat is entered. The following
eats work only with Version 1.1 or later of *The Sims*
d its expansions.

CODE INPUT	DESCRIPTION
utonomy <1-100>	Set free thinking level
ubble_tweak z-offset	Input random large numbers to cause the think bubble to move
raw_all_frames off	Draw all animation disabled
raw_all_frames on	Draw all animation enabled
raw_floorable off	Floorable grid disabled
raw_floorable on	Floorable grid enabled
raw_routes off	Selected person's path hidden
raw_routes on	Selected person's path displayed
enable default	Resets objects to default status
enable objects on/off	Makes stuff invisible
enable status	Checks the status of genable objects in the house
istory	Save family history file
terests	Display personality and interests

CODE INPUT	DESCRIPTION
log_mask	Set event logging mask
map_edit off	Map editor disabled
map_edit on	Map editor enabled
move_objects off	Move any object (off)
move_objects on	Move any object (on)
prepare_lot	Rotates the house and zooms according to your original orientation on the lot
rosebud	1,000 Simoleans
rotation <0-3>	Rotate camera
sim_log begin	Start sim logging
sim_log end	End sim logging
sim_speed <-1000-1000>	Set game speed
sweep off	Ticks disabled
sweep on	Ticks enabled
tile_info off	Tile information hidden
tile_info on	Tile information displayed

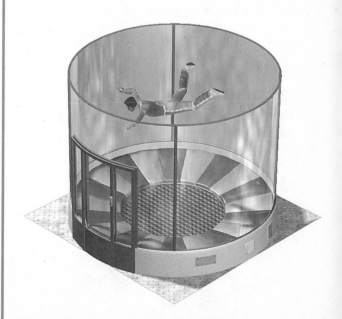

PART II:

CHAPTER 10:
WELCOME TO STUDIO TOWN

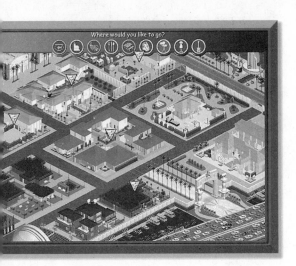

Town Map

NOTE

e "Chapter 11: Almost Famous" for
-depth strategies on becoming a Superstar.

Introduction

It's "Take a Sim to Work Day" in *The Sims Superstar*. After years of watching your favorite Sim disappear into the carpool vehicle, now you can go to work with your Sim and spend hours brushing shoulders with the rich and famous at Studio Town. In this section, we take you on a tour of all nine studio lots, describing the Fame opportunities and services available at each one. Although you can visit the lots in any order, we arranged them to match a typical Fame career sequence. Some Fame objects are available in multiple locations, so your order of progression may vary.

NOTE

All of the directions assume you are standing at the drop-off point, facing the lot.

io Town Fame Objects

	KARAOKE	OPEN MICROPHONE	PHOTO SHOOT	RECORDING STUDIO	TV SET	FASHION RUNWAY	MUSIC VIDEO SET	MOVIE SET
ckingham Galleries	—	—	X	—	—	X	—	—
meron's Lounge	X	X	—	—	—	—	—	—
irchild Film Studios	—	X	—	—	X	—	—	X
ast District	—	—	X	—	—	X	—	—
WLW Studios	—	—	—	—	X	—	—	—
eeker Studios	—	X	—	—	—	—	—	X
idlock Multiplex	X	—	—	X	—	—	—	—
usic for the Eyes	—	—	—	—	—	—	X	—
udio Town Center	X	X	—	—	—	—	—	—

88 Studio Town Drive: Cameron's Lounge

Features

- Open Microphone
- Karaoke Stage
- Billiards, slot machines, pinball
- Food

If you feel luc[ky]
crank the slot
machines a fe[w]
times. When y[ou]
pockets are e[mpty]
join a game o[f]
billiards or pi[nball]
This is a very
busy lounge a[nd]
a great place [to]
make friends.

Cameron's Lounge is a perfect place to launch your singing career or just hang out with other rising stars. The Karaoke Stage is at the lot's far left corner, and the Open Microphone is on the opposite side.

Buy shrimp o[n a]
skewer at the
cart near the
Microphone. [When]
you need the
bathroom, loc[ate]
the stalls at t[he]
back of the lo[unge.]

Studio Town Drive: Studio Town Center

Features

- Open Microphone
- Karaoke Stage
- Shopping
- Food
- Spa

As a not-quite-famous celebrity, Studio Town Center is a perfect place to start your career. It is easy to find in the center of Studio Town. The car deposits your Sim at the beginning of a wide promenade. Follow the path to the opposite end of the lot to reach the Fame objects: the Karaoke Stage on the left and Open Microphone on the right.

NOTE

You can also begin your singing career at Cameron's Lounge, where you can perform at the Karaoke Stage or Open Microphone. Also find Open Microphones at Fairchild Film Studios and Meeker Studios.

After finishing a couple of sets on stage, schmooze with the celebrities until your Motives run down. If your wardrobe needs a little updating, check out the clothing boutique in the front right corner of the lot. A High-Fashion Outfit makes you more appealing to the uppity celebrity types. If you'd rather save your simoleans, quickly change at the dresser located in an alcove behind the interior spiral staircase.

When all that schmoozing leaves your Sim hungry and tired, grab a plate at the Karaoke buffet table, or stop by the sushi bar opposite the Open Microphone.

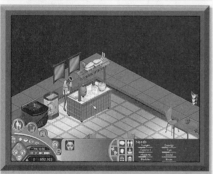

If you have a f͟ simoleans left ͟ shopping at th͟ boutique, buy s͟ nifty movie pos͟ at the kiosks in͟ far left-hand c͟ of the lot.

When nature calls, you have two choices on the ground floor. If the lot is jumpin', use the three bathroom stalls at the spa. However, if a gold toilet is more your style, check out the bathroom attached to the clothing boutique. It's behind a Star Door, so you'll need two or more stars to enter.

As you move u͟ the Fame ladde͟ work on multip͟ celebrity relatio͟ ships at the spa͟ located in the f͟ left-hand sectio͟ the lot. Here yo͟ can languish in͟ baths, soak in a͟ tub, or pay for͟ relaxing massa͟ Conserve Motiv͟ while at Studio͟ Town, but if͟ your active Sim͟ absolutely need͟ a workout to ta͟ the edge off, ju͟ into the pool fo͟ a quick swim.

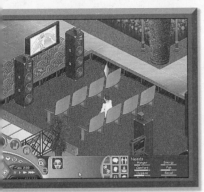

Find cushy sofas on the second floor, but to maximize your downtime, take a seat in the movie theater, where you can gain a little Fun while boosting your Sim's Comfort. The smoothie bar provides light refreshments.

86 Studio Town Drive: Buckingham Galleries

Features

- Photo Shoot: Print Ad, Model
- Fashion Runway
- Shopping
- Food

Just to the right of Studio Town Center is Buckingham Galleries. After earning half a star at the Open Microphone or Karaoke Stage, you unlock the Photo Shoot object on the second floor, where you can pose for a Print Ad (when your Fame advances to two stars, return here for a modeling session). Savvy players will notice the Print Ad is from the *Sims Vacation*! After enduring the bright lights and cameras, chill out and play some computer games.

Take in a fashion show downstairs and dream about strutting your stuff when you unlock the Fashion Runway. If you're not yet qualified to earn simoleans as a model, stop at the boutique and buy a new High-Fashion Outfit.

Food choices are a little thin at Buckingham, but stave off hunger pains with a trip to the sushi bar adjacent to the Fashion Runway.

Don't let your Bladder Motiv[e] too low, becau[se] you're likely t[o] long lines at t[he] only two bath[room] stalls on the l[ower floor].

Dreaming won[t] turn you into a[star,] but if your lov[e life] is a shambles, [you] might want to [make] a wish and tos[s a] coin in the fou[ntain.] It won't chang[e] your luck, but [it's] a fun diversio[n] as you stroll through the lo[bby].

4 Studio Town Drive: Midlock Multiplex

Features

- **Recording Studio: Jingle, Album**
- **Karaoke Stage**
- **Shopping**
- **Food**

When your Sim needs sustenance, look for the double sushi bar directly behind the phone booth. There's never an excuse for a full Bladder, with two multiple-stall bathrooms behind the sushi bars.

Midlock Multiplex is a single-story lot featuring two Recording Studios, located in the far right and midright sections of the lot. With one star under your belt, you can plug in and record a jingle. Later, when you earn three stars, return and cut an album.

Although one star entitles you to record a jingle, you can still step onto the Karaoke Stage and pick up a few simoleans.

A private retreat in the far left-hand corner of the lot features a Mini Trailer, Steam Baths, and Chess Table. You need at least two stars to open the Star Door, although you can sneak in the back way and play chess. However, you will need two stars to enter the Mini Trailer, where you can recharge your Comfort and Bladder Motives.

After earning one-and-a-half stars, visit KWL Studios and fil commercial on set in the lot's right-hand cor Add one more star to your na and you can re to the same se and star in a soap opera.

Working hard in Studio Town can have a devastating effect on the Fun Motive. At Midlock, boost your Sim's score on the basketball court just to the right of the phone booth.

81 Sunrise Boulevard: KWLW Studios

Features

- TV Set: Commercial, Soap Opera
- Shopping
- Food

Although you c find many frills this small, wor set, your Sim's needs are satis A buffet table the lot's far lef hand corner provides quick snacks, and the bathrooms are conveniently located nearby.

Serious actors will love working here, away from the distractions of glitzy spas and computer game stations. When you're done filming, shop at the poster kiosk, or hang around the open area and develop your celebrity and fan Relationships. If all a cab from the phone booth near the TV Set, don't forget to walk to reet, or the cab will take off without you. There's also a phone booth the street.

Studio Town Drive: e Gast District

eatures

Photo Shoot: Model, Print Ad

Fashion Runway

Shopping

Food

Spa

Buckingham Galleries was just a warm-up for your blossoming modeling career, but the Gast District is the big time. This two-story complex has everything for the rich and shallow. If you forgot to don your High-Fashion Outfit before jumping into the limo, stop at the boutique behind the phone booth for a wardrobe upgrade.

To get right to work, walk past the columns in the main promenade, and jump in front of the camera for a photo shoot. If all the bright lights give your Sim the urge to pee, make a pit stop at the bathroom adjacent to the photo set.

NOTE

You can also do a photo shoot at Buckingham Galleries.

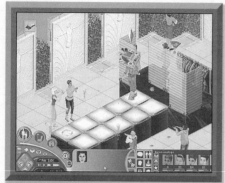

Continuing along the left-hand side of Gast, arrive at the Fashion Runway in the far left corner. After logging three-and-a-half Fame stars, you can model the latest *Sims Superstar* fashions. But a word of warning—runway modeling is not for the faint of heart. The Gast designers can be somewhat indelicate in their critiques. In other words, expect a lot of screaming if you don't perform up to expectations.

Reward yourse[ ] after a tough p[ ] shoot with a vi[ ] the Gast spa in[ ] upper right-ha[ ] corner of the l[ ] The hot tub, m[ ] baths, and stea[ ] provide Fun an[ ] Comfort and opportunities to further your relationships w[ ] local celebrities

If you just can'[ ] pass up a cloth[ ] rack, find anoth[ ] boutique in the[ ] upper right-fro[ ] Even if you're r[ ] interested in shopping, the boutique has a steady stream o[ ] customers, so it[ ] good place to w[ ] on Relationship[ ]

The entire right-hand side of Gast consists of two clothing boutiques. After blowing your daily budget on new threads, take the stairs to the second floor to find more ways to spend your hard-earned simoleans.

The upper left side of Gast houses the only food outlets: a sushi bar and smoothie stand. If you have any Energy left after a long workday, walk to the opposite end of the second floor (front left), and swim with the fishes in the scuba tank.

With four stars worth of Fame, everyone in Studio Town will watch your next career move, so you might as well tease the crowd with your first music video. Find two sets here, both on the first floor along the back wall. A single bathroom stall splits the two sets, so don't wait too long to answer the call, or you might wait in a long line.

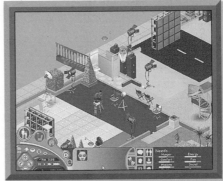

Studio Town Drive: usic for the Eyes Inc.

eatures

Music Video Set
Computer games
Food

Find two buffet tables in the front left-hand section on the first floor. Time your lunch break to share a meal with other celebrities around the large table.

Rounding out the first floor facilities is a small lounge area in the front right-hand section, where you find a single computer for playing games and comfortable seating.

82 Sunrise Boulevard: Fairchild Film Studios

Features
- Movie Set
- Open Microphone
- Food
- Spa

The second floor houses a large bathroom with several stalls in the front left corner. The lone toilet on the first floor is only available to celebrities with at least two stars, so you'll need to streak up the stairs in a Bladder emergency. The only access is the front stairway. A large lounge area stretches behind the bathroom and to the right. Here you can relax and play computer games or listen to music. Spend some of your inflated salary on one of the high-performance gaming stations. The fee is a lofty §35 per session, but your Fun Motive receives an extra boost.

After strolling the red carpet a right and he the corner of building, wher find two Movi Sets. This is th step of your F career. Turn in show-stopping performances befriend the ri celebrities to the final leap superstardom.

NOTE
You can also work on your movie career at Meeker Studios.

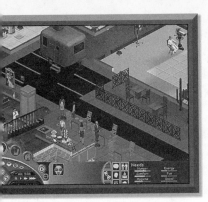

When you get hungry, stop at the buffet table for a catered meal, and then freshen up in the adjacent bathroom. Or if you have at least two stars, step up to the Mini Trailer where you can satisfy Comfort and Bladder Motives in complete privacy. If someone is inside the Mini Trailer, you also get Social Motives.

A big-time star needs big-time pampering, so don't forget about the spa in the lot's far left-hand corner. Here you can soak, steam, or suck up oxygen with the beautiful people.

If you get nostalgic for the good old days of performing in front of hostile audiences, stop by the Open Microphone in the front left-hand section of the second floor. If you'd rather just unwind, walk across to the other side of the second floor, and catch some TV in the theater room.

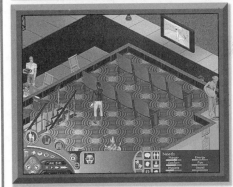

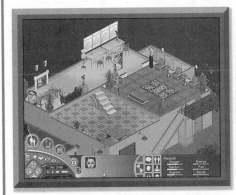

Finally, if all the excitement of Fairchild Film Studios is too much to bear, stroll to the far right-hand section of the upper floor, where you can relax by the fire among friends (or bitter enemies).

83 Sunrise Boulevard: Meeker Studios

Features

- Movie Set
- Open Microphone
- Skydiving Simulator
- Food

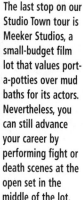

The last stop on our Studio Town tour is Meeker Studios, a small-budget film lot that values port-a-potties over mud baths for its actors. Nevertheless, you can still advance your career by performing fight or death scenes at the open set in the middle of the lot.

Although the facilities are r... sparse, get in ... airtime in the Skydiving Sim... or play compu... games. A food ... buffet keeps y... going, but don... expect cushy c... and sofas. The ... studio trailer i... your best bet f... creature comfo... (if you have at ... least two stars... Finally, and sa... we weren't kidding about ... the port-a-pot...

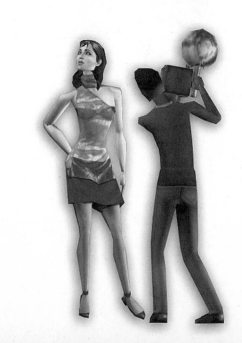

CHAPTER 11: ALMOST FAMOUS

Introduction

Have you ever wanted to jump in the Town Car and look over your Sim Surgeon's shoulder as she completes an emergency appendectomy? Or how about stowing away in the SUV while your Sim Treasure Hunter uncovers the Holy Grail? Well, now you have a chance to participate and manipulate your Sim's career actively on a daily basis. It is exciting, sometimes disappointing, and sometimes unpredictable. In this section we introduce the all-new Fame career. Fame resembles other careers in that you must improve your job skills, expand your circle of friends, and send your Sim to work with a full belly and empty bladder. But there is much more to becoming famous. The following sections describe all the interactions and events you can expect on the Fame career track. For a day-to-day diary of one Sim's drive from Nobody to Superstar, check out "Lights, Camera, Action!"

Getting Started

When you insta[ll] *The Sims Superstar,* Stu[dio] Town appears a[s] a new location [on] the Neighborho[od] screen (just like Downtown in *H[ot] Date* or Vacati[on] Island in *Vacat[ion].* You can go dire[ctly] to Studio Tow[n] without a Sim a[nd] improve any of [the] nine Studio Tow[n] Lots. You can ev[en] bulldoze a lot a[nd] start from scrat[ch] or simply move [a] few objects aro[und] to your liking.

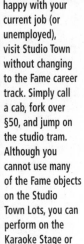

If you are happy with your current job (or unemployed), visit Studio Town without changing to the Fame career track. Simply call a cab, fork over §50, and jump on the studio tram. Although you cannot use many of the Fame objects on the Studio Town Lots, you can perform on the Karaoke Stage or Open Microphone.

When you get tired of singing off-key, spend your hard-earned simoleans on computer games, food carts, mud baths, and a wide variety of other pay-as-you-play objects. Review the "Welcome to Studio Town" section for more information on the services available on each lot.

Of course, you can always save your simoleans and simply follow celebrities around, asking for autographs or hugs (if you feel bold). Some of the Studio Town stars are flattered by your requests and gladly give you autographs. However, keep in mind that celebrities are emotionally fragile, and they can get ugly in the face of over-enthusiastic fans.

NOTE

It is very difficult to build meaningful Relationships with celebrities if you are not famous. It is especially difficult if they have Fame ratings of three stars or higher. However, if you lay the groundwork for several Relationships while you visit, you have a jump start on the Famous Friends requirement when you begin a Fame career.

Although you gain some Comfort by taking breaks on sofas and chairs, or soaking in the hot tub, you cannot restore Energy at Studio Town. So eventually, you need to find a phone booth and call a cab for the trip home. It doesn't cost any simoleans for the return trip home. Time stands still while you visit Studio Town, so you find everything at home, even the time, the same as when you left.

CAUTION

Most phone booths in Studio Town are near the curb where the trams pick up and drop off passengers. If you call a cab from a phone booth on the opposite side of the lot, you need to walk to the pick-up point, or the tram leaves without you.

Launching Your Career

If your visit to Studio Town leaves you filled with envy and desire, perhaps it is your destiny to become famous. When you arrive back home, look for your daily copy of the *Studio Town Insider*, which arrives on the front lawn along with your newspaper. This tinsel-town rag is packed with the inside scoop on everyone who's anyone. For now, it serves a more important purpose—your only source for contacting the SimCity Talent Agency. If your Sim is already gainfully employed, it asks if you want to quit your current job to pursue a Fame career. Say yes, and you can forget about paychecks for a while, at least until your audience decides your singing or acting is worth paying for.

After you snag agent, you are officially on the Fame career tra Get started immediately by calling a cab ar heading for Stu Town. You begi as everyone els does in this city broken dreams a Nobody. Ther no special skill Famous Friends requirements a initial level of F so head straigh the closest Kar Stage or Open Microphone. St Town Center is good place to s but you can fin these Fame obj at several locat

TIP

Although your career is just beginning, it doesn't hurt to pump up your Body, Charisma, and Creativity skills before heading to Studio Town. You need all three skills to advance your career.

If you leap onto the stage and start crooning, your Sim's lack of talent likely inspires a barrage of catcalls from the audience. Before stepping up to the microphone, wander around the room, meeting as many guests as possible. Good conversation builds loyalties, and it never hurts to tip the other performers. After you initiate several friendships, wait until a small crowd gathers near the stage, and then grab the microphone. Select a musical style and let it rip. If you worked

...room sufficiently, the reviews should be favorable. Congratulations! ...are on your way to stardom. Fame, fortune, and shallow relationships ...soon be yours!

TALK TO LANA AT STUDIO TOWN CENTER

Look for Lana, the Studio Town Production Assistant, when you arrive at Studio Town Center. She is easy to recognize, dressed in black and carrying a clipboard. Lana has valuable information on the Fame game, but standing around and waiting for her to answer your questions burns critical seconds, so we include everything she knows right here.

Name Dropping: There are few places quite as informal as the steamy interior of a health spa. In this intimate setting, Sims drop their usual social barriers and talk with just about anyone that happens to be in the spa with them. If you really want to catch their attention, try mentioning the names of celebrities you know. You may hit on a mutual acquaintance and really impress the person you are talking to.

Fame: The more famous you are, the more opportunities that open to you in Studio Town. As you gain Fame, you also gain fans and the attention of other celebrities. Be careful that you don't forsake your fans, lest they cross the fine line between adoration and obsession.

Awards: Three types of awards exist. The first type, and the easiest to achieve, are awards given for excellence in the workplace. Receive these awards through repeated success on the set. The second type is the coveted SIMMY! The SIMMY is only given for outstanding achievement in the Entertainment Industry. One must be really famous to receive this award. Your fans choose the third type of award. If your fans really like you, they may choose to award you with the SimChoice Award—so don't forget about them!

Fans: Fans keep the famous going. Without them, there would be no real reason to be famous. You should talk with your admirers and get to know them if you can. If you were to forget your fans, they would definitely not return the favor. A lack of attention from you is liable to drive at least one of them to be a bit...fixated.

The Pursuit of Fame

After getting your soon-to-be-famous feet wet on the Karaoke Stage, the road to Superstardom gets progressively more difficult. In this section, we explain each aspect of Fame and how it affects your advancement. This is the most important section in the entire strategy guide, because without an understanding of how the system works, the system beats you!

> **TIP** *Vary your initial sequence of styles with each visit to the Photo Shoot, Soap Opera Set, and Recording Booth. If you get lucky and choose the correct order on your first try, you receive a bonus. You earn a decreasing payout of simoleans and Fame points if it takes two or three tries to get it right. The concept is the same on the Fashion Runway, Music Video Set, and Movie Set, with one important difference; you have only two tries to guess the correct sequence. Fortunately, you can earn a partial reward for guessing two of the three styles. In either case, don't forget to write down the results of each sequence, because if you strike out on your last try, the failure will degrade your Fame points (not to mention your self esteem).*

The Fame Track

STARPOWER—DESCRIPTION	FAME OBJECT	CURRENT FAME	FAME REQUIRED TO ADVANCE	FAME AWARDED	FAME PENALTY FOR FAILURE
0—Nobody	Karaoke/Open Mic	1	1	1-2	0
1/2—Stepping Stone	Photo Shoot: Print Ad	2	7	2-3	0
1—Insider	Recording Booth: Jingle	9	12	2-3	0
1 1/2—Name Dropper	Soap Opera Set: Commercial	21	14	3-4	0
2—Studio Fly	Photo Shoot	35	17	4-6-7	-8
2 1/2—Sell Out	Soap Opera	52	26	5-7-8	-10
3—Trendsetter	Recording Booth	78	78	8-12-20	-15
3 1/2—Player	Fashion Runway	156	144	25-25-40	-20
4—Talk of the Town	Music Video	300	250	35-50-60	-30
4 1/2—Celebrity	Movie Set	550	350	55-70-80	-50
5—Superstar	Superstardom!	900			

*When you're at 0–4 1/2 stars, Fame decay starts only if you miss one day of work. When you're at 5 stars, Fame decay is daily regardless of whether you make your presence at Studio Town or not.

rpower/Description

Ten levels exist between Nobody and Superstar, with each level valued at half a star. Your stars are displayed on the Job menu, directly under Fame. Besides tracking your career advancement, Starpower also influences your

...ty to meet other celebrities. Studio Town has a definite caste system, and ...rities prefer to hang with others of similar stature. So, as you move up ...charts, pay attention to your Starpower, and make friends with other ...rities in reach of your current standing. This isn't a hard and fast rule; so ...u want to introduce yourself to a Superstar as a Nobody, knock yourself ...But, don't be surprised if you are summarily dismissed.

E ME	FAMOUS FRIENDS REQUIRED	CHARISMA/BODY/ CREATIVITY REQUIRED
...s	0	0/0/0
...0	0	1/0/1
...5	0	2/1/2
...0	0	3/2/3
...00	2	4/3/4
...50	4	6/4/4
...00	7	6/5/6
...25	11	7/6/7
...25	14	8/7/8
...50	18	10/8/9

Fame Objects

A way to earn Fame is to perform successfully on one of the Music, Acting, or Fashion Fame objects. Signing autographs and getting your picture taken by the Paparazzo also brings small amounts of Fame. Fame objects are scattered among the nine Studio Lots in Studio Town. With the exception of the Karaoke Stage and Open Microphone, which are available at the start of the Fame career, subsequent objects unlock as you advance through the levels. However, your Fame level does not lock you to an object. You can continue to use Fame objects you used at the beginning of your Fame track even when you're a Superstar. For example, when you reach three stars, the Soap Opera Commercial becomes available. To advance to three-and-a-half stars, you must achieve sufficient Fame at the Soap Opera Commercial (along with satisfying the other requirements for advancement), thus opening up the next Fame object, Photo Shoot Set. This process continues until you become a Superstar.

Current Fame

This number represents a hidden tabulation of Fame points achieved when you reach a level. You don't see this total in the game, but it is an ever-changing figure that reflects successes, failures, and decays (see the following).

Fame Required to Advance

Once again, this is a hidden number that represents the amount of Fame points required to advance to the next level. Note the dramatic increase in the number of Fame points needed at the higher levels.

Fame Awarded

How well you do on a particular Fame object determines the number of hidden Fame points your Sim earns. This formula varies depending on the object. Two types of Fame objects exist. For explanation purposes we call them Class I and Class II interactions. Class I interactions—including the Karaoke Stage; Open Microphone; Photo Shoot: Print Ad; Recording Booth: Jingle; and Soap Opera Commercial— simply require your Sim to show up and perform a task. At the Karaoke Stage and Open Microphone, Fame points are awarded based on how well the audience receives your performance. If you sufficiently prep the crowd, you get rave reviews, and correspondingly, the highest number of Fame points. The lower number is awarded for a moderately successful audience response.

You perform the Photo Shoot: Print Ad, Recording Booth: Jingle, and Soap Opera Commercial in front of a director or producer rather than a live audience. Your award is based on a complex formula that involves Mood, and you receive either the higher or lower number of Fame points.

The Class II Fame interactions inc Photo Shoot, S Opera, Recordir Booth, Fashion Runway, Music Video, and Mov Set. These obje are interactive, meaning that y must make decisions on yo acting, singing, modeling style. The first Class II interaction is Photo Shoot, which unlock after you earn two stars.

When performi the Photo Shoo Soap Opera, an Recording Boot you have three opportunities t select a sequen of three styles. This means it is impossible to f (unless you do keep track of y choices on each

You receive the highest Fame award if you guess the sequence on the fir attempt. If it takes two tries, you receive the middle payout. If you don't guess the sequence until the third try, you earn the smallest Fame award However, the good news is that you can eventually earn enough Fame po to move to the next level even if it takes three tries to achieve success. It just takes you a little longer to accumulate the necessary Fame points for advancement.

The last group of Class II Fame interactions— Fashion Runway, Music Video, and Movie Set—are more difficult because you need a considerable amount of luck to succeed. Instead of three chances to choose the correct sequence, have only two attempts. This means you are not guaranteed success by ess of elimination. Naturally, the Fame payout is highest if you guess the er sequence on your first try. The middle Fame award is for guessing the ence on your second try. The lowest Fame payout is for guessing two out ree. If you only get one correct choice after two tries, it is considered a e, and you receive a Fame penalty (see the following section).

CAUTION

ep your Sim's Mood above 0 and Energy otives above -85, or they refuse to use the ss II Fame interactions (Photo Shoot, Soap era, Recording Booth, Fashion Runway, usic Video, and Movie Set).

e Penalty for Failure

After a few trips down the Fashion Runway or sessions in the Recording Booth, you will get used to receiving immediate, and often emotional, responses to your work. Obviously, it is more fun for a designer to blow kisses at you rather

jumping up and down, shaking a fist in your direction. If you have the rtunate experience of missing an entire sequence or making only one ect choice, your Sim receives a Fame penalty (from -8 on the Photo Shoot 0 on the Movie Set) to go with your public tongue lashing.

NOTE

No Fame penalty exists for failure on the Class I Fame interactions mentioned above. However, the SimCity Talent Agency watches your performance very closely, and it only takes a few flops for them to degrade your Starpower.

Daily Decay

Aside from Fame penalties, you also risk Daily Decay if you don't spend enough time at Studio Town. When your Sim has from 0–4.5 stars, Daily Decay begins when you miss two straight days. Here is how the internal system works. Each day at around 3:00 P.M., the game checks to see if you went to Studio Town that day. If you didn't, your Sim receives a hidden check mark. If you go to Studio Town the next day, the check mark disappears, and your Sim's record is clear. However, if you miss a second consecutive day, your Sim receives another second check mark, which triggers the Daily Decay listed in the table. As soon as you go back to Studio Town, all check marks disappear and you are back at square one.

CAUTION

If you fail to visit Studio Town for three straight days, you receive a call from your agent, reminding you to pay more attention to your career. If you don't show up for six consecutive days, your agent drops you, which immediately takes you out of the Fame track. If you sign up again, you start from the bottom—as a Nobody. On the Fame track, you can visit Studio Town a maximum of once per day. No limit exists to the number of visits when you are a tourist.

> ### NOTE
>
> *When you reach five stars, Daily Decay occurs regardless of whether or not your Sim visits Studio Town.*

Base Income

This figure represents the standard pay for successfully using a Fame object. You can earn more if you complete the sequence on the first try. Another way to earn more than the base amount is to use a Fame object again, even after you qualify for the next object. The higher Star level earns you this bonus. However, the tradeoff is that you earn fewer Fame points, and if you linger in the past too long, some may perceive you as a slacker. When you reach four-and-a-half or five stars and you need to build up your bank account, you can use the Fashion Runway over and over again. You earn less Fame, but there are no penalties.

Famous Friends Required

This is arguably the most difficult aspect of your rise to Superstardom, especially when you top three stars. This number represents your Famous Friends' combined Starpower (not the actual number of friends, as in other *Sims* careers). Frequently check the Work menu to keep tabs on your current status. Adding to the challenge is the ever-changing status of *all* Studio Town celebrities. Each day two celebrities experience changes in their Starpower. This occurs randomly among all the celebrities, so it can have a positive or negative impact on your Famous Friends' collective Starpower. This is a good reason to develop a few extra Famous Friendships, even after you reach your current requirement. Study the next section "The Art of Schmoozing" for a wealth of information on making and keeping Famous Friends.

Charisma/Body/Creativity Required

Required work s are a carryover traditional *Sims* careers, and the *Sims Supersta* priorities are Charisma, Body, Creativity. Takin day off now an then from the Studio Town gri is required for improving your skills and maintaining Famous Friendships, so don't become a fame-aholi or your career may grind to a halt.

> ## IMPROVING YOUR FAME SKILLS
>
> - **Charisma: Medicine Cabinet, Mirrors (practicing speech); Bard Bust (reciting soliloquy)**
> - **Body: Exercise machines, swimming pool, Skydiving Simulator**
> - **Creativity: Easel, piano**

wards

Aside from monetary rewards, Studio Town presents the following awards for outstanding achievement:

- Performance Awards: These awards are presented in each of the three Fame paths: Music, Acting, and Fashion. Trophies include Bronze, Silver, and Gold, and you receive them for outstanding work in one field.

- The SIMMY: After you earn two-and-a-half stars, you are eligible to earn a SIMMY

ugh it is rare to receive one if your Fame level is under four stars). It
te a treat, as a stretch limo pulls up with a celebrity presenter and
razzi inside. Your Sim dons formal wear and accepts the award at the
Be sure to store your SIMMY in a safe place to keep it out of the hands
e greedy Obsessed Fan (see "The Price of Fame" later in this section for
information on this disturbed soul).

Choice Award: The only way to earn this prize is to lavish attention and
dness on your fans. You need to take regular time off from schmoozing
h the beautiful people to build rapport with your fan base. This means
arding autograph seekers who wait patiently for you to finish your
ebrity conversations.

Chance Cards

Just when you think your career is in high gear, along comes a random event to bring you back down to earth. After you reach one-and-a-half stars, you can receive a call from your agent with good news or bad news. The good news comes in the form of an endorsement that puts a bundle of simoleans in your pocket. Even more exciting than simoleans is a phone call telling you that your star is on the rise and that everyone in Studio Town wants to be your friend. This

translates into a significant boost to all your celebrity Relationship scores.

Now for the bad news. You can expect a debit from your bank account if your agent must bail you out of an uncomfortable situation. Other phone calls can be devastating to your career advancement, especially if your

agent informs you that celebrities walk the other way when you arrive at
Studio Town. If this happens, plan on spending a good deal of time mending
your falling Relationship scores.

Paparazzo

What would celebrity life be without an annoying photographer in your Sim's face? The Paparazzo snaps pictures, but only if he deems you worthy of the price of film. You can approach the Paparazzo and "Pose for a Picture" or "Stage a Publicity Stunt." The latter choice is more likely to garner a photograph, but in either case, the Fame boost is minimal. However, when your Fame surpasses four-and-a-half stars, or if your career receives

a recent Fame boost (at least 30 points since your last arrival at Studio Town), the Paparazzo may take your picture as you exit your limousine at curbside.

You can also entice the Paparazzo to take pictures if you stage a Publicity Event with another celebrity. This is usually a fake fight that unfolds very quickly, so make sure the Paparazzo is in the vicinity before you put on the show. However, there is no guarantee the Paparazzo will deem the stunt worthy of a shot.

Find the Papara strolling aroun Studio Town lot spends most of time looking fo pictures rather taking them, b he responds to newsworthy ev which can inclu a passionate ki between your Sim and anoth celebrity, or a seemingly innocent hot tub session with another hot Stud Town property. On the home front, you can always count on the Paparazz accompany the celebrity presenter when your Sim receives a SIMMY Awa

Of course, the Paparazzo love cover tragedie including your very own Nerv Breakdown. If career and life fall apart on t set, the Papara will snap away publicizing yo collapse and further demoli your Fame.

> # NOTE
>
> *If the Paparazzo takes your picture, be sure to check the tabloid the next day and see whether you made the news.*

e Price of Fame

e Obsessed Fan

During the early part of your career, the pursuit of Fame seems easy enough. You do a few gigs on stage, pose for a Print Ad, hang out with the stars in Studio Town; life is good. But midway through your climb to the top, things start to change.

earning two-and-a-half stars, your strolls through the lot seem more
ult, with clusters of fans milling about, hanging on your every word. This
turning point—when you must decide to be the people's star or just
er celebrity.

All it takes to keep your public happy is to build a total of 126 Relationship points with an entire fan base of 18. This could be 18 fans with 7 points; or two fans, one with 60 and the other with 66. If you fall below this level

n you have two-and-a-half stars or above), the Obsessed Fan appears.

Obnoxious doesn't even begin to describe this guy. He is like something sticky on the bottom of your shoe. Wherever you go, the Obsessed Fan follows—to the bathroom, on the set, to the dinner table. He does not directly engage in any activities with your Sim; but he is always present, staring, jumping up and down, clenching his fists, and taking photographs.

Aside from being an annoyance, the Obsessed Fan can do some damage, especially at night when everyone in your house is asleep (including pets). He wanders around the property looking for award trophies, so never leave them outside. There is a slight chance the Obsessed Fan will enter your house looking for awards, so don't leave them in obvious places on the ground floor either.

Your only recou for directly dea with the Obses Fan is to "Bera him or tell him "Go Away." Thi feels good, but rarely makes h leave (you hav a 1 in 10 chanc of success).

Fortunately, yo have another o at Studio Town Lana, the Studi Town Assistant ask her to "Sh the Obsessed Fan. She usuall responds quick But keep in mi that the game checks for Obs Fan conditions

hour, so he will return unless you attend to your fan base and raise your Relationship score above 125.

TIP

A foolproof trick for protecting your valuable trophies is to keep them in a room accessible only by a Star Door.

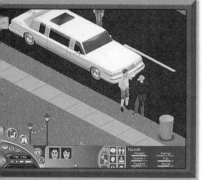

At home hire a Butler, who keeps the Obsessed Fan away during working hours (7 A.M.–Midnight). Of course, the Butler has many other worthwhile functions, including cooking, cleaning, keeping appliances repaired, and dismissing unwanted guests. But it is worth his daily salary of §500 to see him slap the Obsessed Fan and send him slinking off your property.

Nervous Breakdown

Every time you completely fail at the Music Recording Booth, Soap Opera Set, Photo Shoot, Music Video Set, Fashion Runway, or Movie Set, the game gives your Sim an invisible checkmark. Don't worry about the consequences, as long as your successful performances outnumber your bad ones.

However, if you have a run of bad luck on the set, you run the risk of giving your Sim a Nervous Breakdown. This is not a pretty sight. Aside from falling apart in front of your peers and fans, your Sim suffers a drop in Comfort, Fun, and Bladder Motives and loses some Fame points. Depending on where your Sim is on the scale, this could trigger a drop in Starpower.

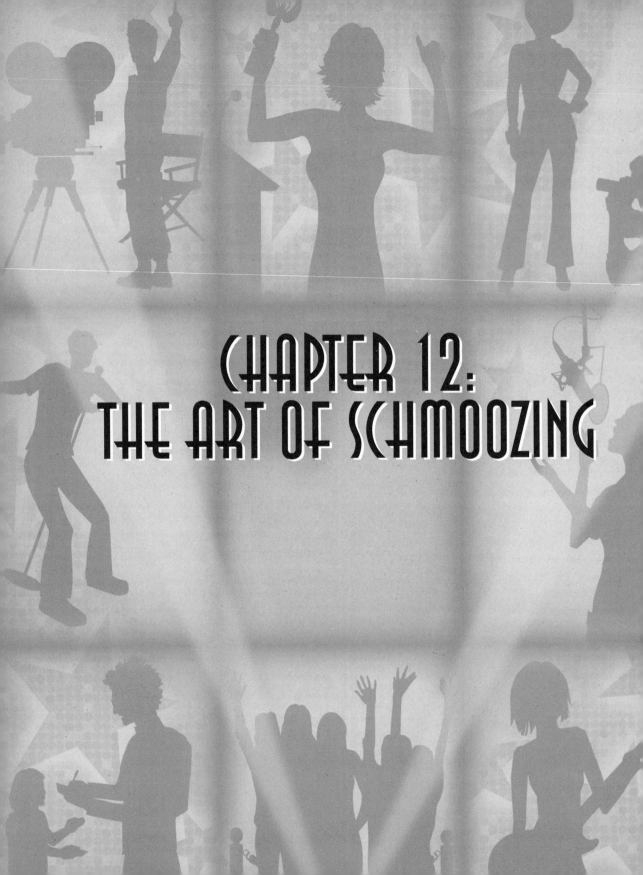

CHAPTER 12:
THE ART OF SCHMOOZING

Introduction

veteran *Sims* players know all about friends. The original game, and every expansion pack since then, presented new challenges in finding and maintaining quality Relationships. As you might expect, Famous Friends have plenty of issues. If you thought hanging out with the Goths was tough, wait until you hang with Trendsetters, Radio Flys, and Name Droppers. In this section, we teach you the art of schmoozing, with tips for finding, meeting, and coddling your ever-fragile Famous Friends.

NOTE

If you are a Sims newbie, check out the first half of this book for exhaustive information and general strategies on boosting your Relationship scores.

UNDERSTANDING CELEBRITY ~~FRIENDS'~~ STARPOWER

When it comes to satisfying career Relationship requirements, two very important distinctions set *The Sims Superstar* apart from all other *Sims* titles. In a traditional Sims career, a Family Friends requirement exists. As the title suggests, this allows every member of the household to contribute their friends to the total. For example, a level 10 position as Mayor in the Politics Career track, requires seventeen friends. Everyone in the house, including the employed Sim, spouses, and children, can satisfy this total. **In *The Sims Superstar, only your character's Famous Friends count toward satisfying a level requirement.** Your spouse may have Famous Friends, but they do not count toward your total.

The second critical difference is in how the friends total is calculated. In a traditional Sims career, Family Friends are compiled as a head count. A requirement of seventeen friends, means seventeen different friends. **However, in *The Sims Superstar,* the Total Starpower of your Famous Friends, rather than a head count is what's important.** Hence, if you have five Famous Friends and each one has a Starpower of 3, your Friends' Total Starpower is 15. So, although you may keep the same number of Famous Friends throughout the game, the Total Starpower may go up or down due to changes in their "individual" Starpower ratings. Understanding the dynamics behind Friends' Total Starpower is the key to meeting your level requirements as you move toward Superstardom.

The New Kid on the Lot

Studio Town celebrities are a tightly knit and tightly wound group. They tend to hang with Sims of like stature in the industry. Of course, this makes it incredibly difficult for a Nobody who just wants to make friends. When you first arrive at Studio Town, step onto the curb, and watch the parade of cars and limos as they drop off their pampered passengers. You should have excellent results introducing yourself to celebrities who emerge from the white carpool car (0–1/2 stars). After earning your first half star, immediately move up to the black limo passengers (1–2 1/2 stars).

Limo Passengers

- **White Carpool Car: 0–1/2 Stars**
- **Black Limo: 1–2 1/2 Stars**
- **White Limo: 3–4 1/2 Stars**
- **Pink Limo: 5 Stars**

Now that you' a celebrity on rise, don't act too much like drooling fan. I okay to tell a celebrity "I'm Biggest Fan!" don't get carri away; and by means, pick yo spots for thro yourself on th ground and declaring "I'm Not Worthy!"

Keep things ni and light until build up a sco 30. By this tim the celebrity i probably look the exit. Keep going if you c don't harass t celebrity to a at which your Relationship s starts droppin

With a 30-point base, you can invite the celebrity to your house, where can set up various group activities to boost the Relationship to the nex

You can build up a Daily Relationship score as high as 70 or 80 on your first visit, and if your Starpower is similar to that of the celebrity, you may even make a Family Friend. But this is not the norm, so we recommend laying the groundwork at ...dio Town and then solidifying the friendship with a home-cooked group ...al, a game of billiards, and some TV.

If you decide to throw caution to the wind and go after a big-time star, you have very few choices for social interaction. Hence, the target celebrity quickly becomes bored with "I'm Your Biggest Fan!" and "Were you in the tabloids?" If you keep repeating these interactions, the celebrity gets very frustrated, and you may even find your Relationship score falling into negative territory. A better technique is to use frequent, brief encounters to build the Relationship score gradually, eventually unlocking new interactions.

CAUTION

...emember that the scores you see on the ...elationships panel reflect how your Sim feels ...bout the celebrity. Your score may climb as ...igh as one hundred, but until the celebrity ...arts warming up, he or she may still not ...onsider your Sim a friend. This may take two ...r three visits, especially if the celebrity's ...tarpower is considerably higher than yours.

TIP

When your Starpower is nonexistent, it is difficult to get celebrities to stop and talk to you in Studio Town. Make your Sim more appealing by wearing a High-Fashion Outfit. Also, it helps to have a good "Body," so spend some time in the pool or on the weight bench to make your Sim more attractive to the already beautiful people of Studio Town.

A good place to break the ice with Celebrities, and boost your Social Motive, is at a dining table. You have better luck conversing with strangers during a meal than just plopping down next to a celebrity on a sofa. If you use the ...et tables, you'll get even more talk time due to the faster service. Most ...he Studio Town lots include dining areas with tables, although one of the ...gest is at the Gast District, where a food service area stretches the entire ...th of the second floor. The scuba tank on one end is also a big draw, so ...g around near the door to catch celebrities on their way out.

Group Activities

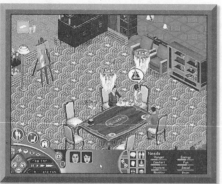

When a celebrity accepts an invitation to your house, you can control the interactions much more, and if you carefully stage the events, you can quickly build your Relationship score. First and foremost, make sure there's plenty of fresh food on the counter. Celebrities are no different than other Sims. They love to eat almost immediately on entering your house.

After eating, Celebrities often go straight to the bathroom, which provides a good opportunity for staging the next activity. Turn on the TV, start playing billiards, jump into the hot tub, or just turn on some music and start dancing.

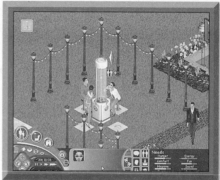

As your bank account builds, can afford mor expensive grou activity items, including the s objects availab at Studio Town Energize! Oxyg Bar is an excell group activity up to four gues and it provides strong satisfact (7) for the Fun Motive. The ho is always a goo choice for grou activities. Make sure your Sim's Motives are in the green befor entering, to ensure a length session with yo Famous Friend.

The spa at Studio Town Center is a veritable hotbed of celebrity group activity. You can find spa objects at other lots, but the Studio Town Center is the biggest and often the busiest. Check out the hot tub, steam baths, and oxygen bar. Users of these objects also interact with one another, not just with other Sims using the same object. This is unique to the spa, and these objects do not interact in the same way if you place them in your home.

Staging Photo Ops

Another reason to develop Famous Friendships is to stage Photo Ops and Publicity Events. These events improve your Relationship score with a celebrity, and a successful Photo Op adds to your Fame, especially if your Famous Friends has a higher Starpower. It is not guaranteed that the Paparazzi will take your picture, but when he does, it's more than worth the effort.

Checking the Tabloid

When you achieve three-and-a-half stars, regularly check the "Who's Hot in Studio Town?" list in the tabloid to see where you should direct your social efforts. It also gives you a preview of who's on the way up—and who could drop off the list.

TIP

...you have trouble making Famous Friends, ... this long-term strategy: Create other ...milies in the neighborhood with Sims on the ...me career track. Develop their careers until ...ey climb higher up the pecking order than ...ur Sim, and then go back to your original ...aracter. Look out for celebrity neighbors ...ho just happen to stroll by your door. If you ...spond quickly, you can greet them and then ...vite them inside for a snack. They may be ...ol to your advances at first, but after a while, ...ey'll be draining your beverage bar and ...aking in your hot tub; and most importantly, ...mping up your Friends' Total Starpower.

Prima's Official Strategy Guide

Fan Relationships

With all the pressures of establishing Famous Friendships, you can easily overlook the loyal fans who flock to Studio Town just to get a glimpse of you climbing out of the limo. You can achieve Superstardom without being respectful to your fans, but at what price? If you fail to pay the slightest attention to the "other people" at Studio Town, you run the risk of being perpetually harassed by the Obsessed Fan (see "The Price of Fame" section for more information). You only need a total of 126 Relationship points with your entire fan base to keep the Obsessed Fan away, so it pays to sign a few autographs and shake a few hands on the way to the top.

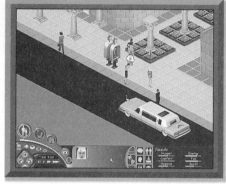

Fans wander a
over Studio To
and during the
early stages o'
Fame career, t
hardly notice y
But after you
achieve two-a
a-half stars,
everything cha
While you talk
another celeb
you may notic
fan jumping u
down, hoping
autograph. Yo
see your Sim's
in their thoug
bubbles, and i
short order, yo
activity queue
will be filled
with requests.
Remember, all
takes is a little
time to keep t
Obsessed Fan
from coming o
of his hole.

CHAPTER 13:
LIGHTS, CAMERA, ACTION!

Introduction

Up until now, we reviewed the most critical ingredients of the Fame career path. However, your life as a celebrity has many aspects, and the best way to experience them is to tag along with our Sims as they work up the Studio Town Hot List. The following sections take you through a typical *Sims Superstar* career, from Nobody all the way to Superstar.

Our First Trip to Studio Town

There's nothing like holding up the studio tram for a goofy picture. It's fun to entice the Paparazzo to use his camera, but he doesn't give you a lot of Fame. At the lower levels, every little bit helps. It will be difficult to get him to take your picture when you're a Nobody, unless you have high Body or Creativity skills. Later we'll look for a well-known star and stage a juicy Publicity Stunt.

After taking th[…] to Studio Tow[…] pick the Midlo[…] Multiplex for […] musical debut […] the Karaoke S[…] Having Creativ[…] skills is essen[…] getting good reviews. The fi[…] attempt behin[…] microphone is […] disaster, so we[…] prime the cro[…] before our sec[…] set. After a lit[…] hand-shaking and idle chatt[…] we receive a smattering of applause from[…] audience of on[…] Hey, it's a star[…]

After figuring out the value of working the crowd, our nex[…] performance is […] smash success. […] like me; they re[…] like me! At the Karaoke Stage, […] tips multiply by[…] number of hap[…] listeners, so the[…] bigger the cro[…]

the bigger the paycheck. Most of the crowd is dressed casually, but we s[…] a couple of High-Fashion Outfits, which usually means celebrities. And th[…] voluptuous blonde in the pink dress; isn't that…?

AUTION

gative reviews at the Open Microphone
d Karaoke Stage do not affect your Sim's
me points. However, as you advance through
e Fame track, too many failed performances
n put your Sim at risk for a Nervous Breakdown.

NOTE

Just a reminder: Fame points are not *visible* in the game. This is an internal system of tracking your Sim's progress through the Fame career. See the "Almost Famous" chapter for a detailed explanation of how Fame points work, including a table with values for each level.

After the performance, we single out a celebrity type for our first Famous Friend. We decide to latch onto this poor lady for as long as we can stand up—or at least until she walks away in disgust. Our Motives are

ng low, but we have just enough for one more round of Karaoke.

The Camera Loves You (You Hope!)

After a few good sets on the Karaoke Stage, we receive our first promotion to a half star, or what is commonly referred to in Studio Town as a Stepping Stone.

On the way to the Photo Shoot, we run into a famous recording star. Our current Fame status is Stepping Stone, so we are certainly not beneath asking for an autograph. Amazingly, we even have a fan of our own! This is a good opportunity to build the collective fan Relationship score in the hopes of discouraging the Obsessed Fan from showing his greasy face.

Back at the home front, we spend a little time with our spouse, who has been neglected since beginning the Fame track. A little swing dancing keeps our Sim's Social Motive high. After a good night's sleep,

meal, and a shower, we'll try our hand at the Photo Shoot: Print Ad.

It's time for our first Photo Shoot: Print Ad, but first we must change out of our pajamas. On our next visit, do this at home to save precious time (and Motives).

After a few positive reviews at the Photo Shoot and some more schmoozing with the local celebrities, we take a cab back home to celebrate our latest promotion to one star: Insider. That High-Fashion Outfit feels so good, we keep it on for a quick game of billiards before turning in for the night.

Jingle All the Way

Our first atten recording a Jir is uninspiring, after a second spin in the bo the director is encouraged. A a few more se in the booth, C nails it. Our Si Mood affects success in the Recording Boo we decide to l Studio Town ea for some rest socializing at h We don't need Famous Friend until we reach stars, but it's too early to bu Relationships.

The Cameras Finally Roll!

After earning o and-a-half stars can call our Sim Name Dropper. Finally, we can leave the world Karaoke, Photo Shoots, and Jin behind and mov to the bright lig of television, w a bona fide TV Commercial. Wh our Charisma (3), Body (2), and Creativity (3) skills are sufficient for the n promotion, we send our Sim off in a black limo (no more carpool, thank y to KWLW Studios, where we film a commercial on the Soap Opera Set. Or day we'll come back here as a big-time star!

oking Good Is Not Enough

After achieving two stars, our Studio Fly sets off to Buckingham Galleries for the first job as a highly paid model. We don't have enough experience for the Fashion Runway, but we can finally do more than just stand around and look pretty. As a Photo Shoot: Model, select a sequence of three styles that places our outfit in the best possible light.

The photographer tells us in no uncertain terms that our first attempt was off the mark. Fortunately, we have three tries to get it right; although the longer it takes, the less we get paid, both in simoleans and Fame points. It takes three tries, but we finally nail it, and the photographer reluctantly offers praise for our efforts. It takes at least three successful Photo Shoots to earn our promotion to two-and-a-half stars, at which time we earn the right to be called a complete Sellout!

We're Halfway There

After earning two-and-a-half stars, it's off to the Soap Opera Set for our first dramatic role. We are just one promotion away from existing in the upper half of all celebrities in Studio City. Along with this notoriety comes a new responsibility

to pay attention to our fans regularly. At two-and-a-half stars, the game checks fan Relationships every hour, and if we don't have a total of at least 126 Relationship points, the Obsessed Fan rears his ugly head.

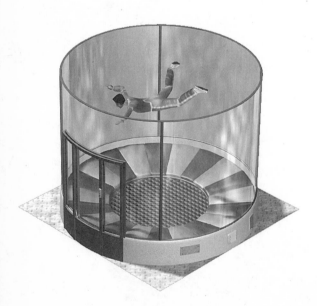

From the Phot Shoot to the S Opera Set, the Famous Friend requirement j from two to f so we do a lit schmoozing b stepping onto set. A visit to spa at Studio Center is just ticket. The bat full of celebri and there's no like a tub full mud to lighter the atmospher Unfortunately, Sim suffers a social setback he tries to smo big-time star. I she didn't soa long enough.

We make a concerted effo to find more traditional wa make friends, as the dining table at a stud cafeteria. Afte eating and tal our fill, we co the unhappy recipient of ou kiss near the p kiosks and line up with a bun social interacti She seems receptive, but can't forget th waiting patient the backgroun a moment of o valuable, yet superficial tim

It's time to take our place among the Studio City immortals. The first scene on the Soap Opera Set goes well. We need three takes to get it right, but it's a start, and our Fame points are on the rise.

Why Me?

I guess we should have paid more attention to those autograph seekers. Just as we wrap the Soap Opera scene, the Obsessed Fan drops in to visit. We head for the phone booth, stopping just long enough to enlist Lana's help in getting rid of the Obsessed Fan, so we can sign a few autographs in peace.

Prima's Official Strategy Guide

The Obsessed Fan is like a bad penny. Fortunately, berating works (a rare occurrence), and he leaves long enough for us to invite a guest for dinner. But we know he'll come back, and most likely, the berating tactic will not work.

Even our garbage isn't safe.

As bad as the Obsessed Fan is, he really can't derail your career. We decide to put up with him for now and concentrate on today's lines. We nail the scene, and the SimCity Talent Agency informs us of a promotion to three stars. It's time to cut a record!

CAUTION

Before entering the Soap Opera Set (or any other Fame object that requires a series of decisions), make sure to set your game speed setting to normal. At the higher speeds, you can easily miss the director's response to each of the three scenes.

Why Don't They Love Me Anymore?

As we scratch and claw our way up the ladder of Fame, we painfully realize our success often depends on the success of our Famous Friends. It seems that two of our nearest and dearest fell out of favor with the decision-makers in Studio Town, and they fell off the "Who's Hot in Studio Town?" along with our This is a good reminder to expand our social circle so we can better absorb these bumps in the road to Fame. We head to Cameron's Lounge where the joint is always jumpin'. In no time, we have our eyes on a new friend, and the early conversation goes as smooth as silk.

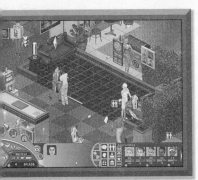

There is plenty to do at Cameron's. After our new Famous Friend leaves the lot, we meet a fan and shoot some darts until it's time to drag our exhausted Sim to the phone booth to call the limo.

...ying Down Some Tracks

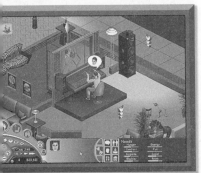

After restoring our Famous Friends to seven (the minimum for our next promotion), we step into the booth to record our album. The producer loves our style, and we pick three perfect choices for our first session. Our Sim receives a handsome bonus for hitting it on the first try. Even the Obsessed Fan can't spoil the moment!

It's all good. We receive a call that our star is truly on the rise and that everyone is clamoring to get next to our famous Sim. This is one of several chance cards that periodically come up, and fortunately, this one is positive. All our Famous Friends' Relationships receive a small, but welcome boost.

We pause at our old Karaoke hangout to sign a few autographs. Remember that famous recording artist? Sorry; we have no time for her now.

As career demands take their toll on our free time, we decide to bite the bullet and hire a Butler for a lofty §500 a day. The good fellow pays immediate dividends during a social gathering by the pool when he confronts the Obsessed Fan.

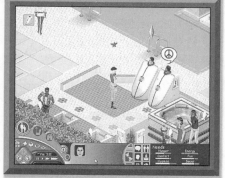

We decide to take a day off from our busy schedule to seek out new friends. Our first stop is Cameron's Lounge, where everyone seems to be in a good mood. As our Sim gets tired, we call for the limo and head over to the Studio Town Center for some spa schmoozing. Once again, we are too busy (and too steamy) to pay attention to the local rock star.

Walk This Way

After mastering Recording Booth few more times, sachet over to t Fashion Runway our first experie the pressure-pa world of high-fa modeling. At thr and-a-half stars, Sim is a Player and the stakes a considerably hig The Fashion Run is the first of th Fame objects tha provide only tw opportunities to guess the three-sequence. Some is involved here, gear up for a lon learning curve. T early reviews are not favorable, as the resident designer waves fan in disgust.

Our second tour the runway begin where we left of the toilet. But in we get the hang and before long designer is frolic behind the glass.

Dance Fever

Like the Fashion Runway, we have only two tries to guess the sequence for our first Music Video. But the director is waving her hands with glee, so we must be doing something right.

After several successful Fashion Runway sessions, we finally qualify for a promotion. Next up for our new four-star Talk of the Town is a Music Video.

Despite our early success, we settle in for the long haul. We must practically double our Fame points to earn the next promotion to four-and-a-half stars and unlock the final Fame object—the Movie Set.

Ready for Your Close-Up, Mr. Sim?

This is it, the final step to Superstar. At four-and-a-half stars, our celebrity is ready to make the final jump. We can choose "Death Scene" or "Fight Scene." We've been pumping a little iron lately, so our Sim opts for the action. With swords flashing, give the director something to cheer about.

The Death Scene is almost too emotional to watch, except for the Obsessed Fan, who thinks we're doing a comedy. With tears flowing, we make a believer out of the director.

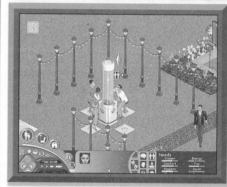

The last step to Superstar takes time, and there simply no way to rush the process. You must work on the Movie Set, building your Fame points, while maintaining 18 combined Family Friends Starpower. While you make that long, hard, climb, enjoy the fruits of your labor. As a celebrity, you earn a whopping §750 per successful performance (more if you pick the sequence on the first try). Now you can afford some of life's little pleasures, such as a backyard Scuba Tank and Oxygen Bar.

TIP

If you need money after unlocking the Movie Set, go back to the Fashion Runway. You'll earn less Fame, but more money than you did before. The Music Video Set is another good alternative: Less money than the Fashion Runway, but more Fame.

CHAPTER 14: NEW OBJECTS

Introduction

Sims Superstar includes over 120 new objects available in Buy and Build Modes when you occupy a house. In this section, objects are arranged by category as they appear on the Buy Mode menus (Seating, Surfaces, Decorative, and so on), with pictures, prices, and ratings (if applicable). The Efficiency Value (1–10) indicates how well an item satisfies its related Motive, with a higher number rating more for your Sims.

NOTE

"Studio Town Only," later in this section, includes objects available only when you are on a Community Lot in Studio Town.

SUPERSTAR Objects

Seating

Dining Chairs

Caveat Emptor Folding Chair

Cost: §125

Motive: Comfort (2)

Wool/Fiberglass/Chromalume Chair

Cost: §235

Motive: Comfort (3)

Liberty's Choice Dining Chair

Cost: §335

Motive: Comfort (3)

Chrome Dive Bar Chair

Cost: §500

Motives: Comfort (4), Room (1)

...nge Chairs

...are Peg Easy Chair

Cost: §629

Motive: Comfort (7)

...ply Modern Leather Chair

Cost: §1,702

Motives: Comfort (9), Room (2)

...as

...ited Edition Sternwood Boxer Cordelan Sofa

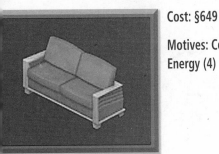

Cost: §649

Motives: Comfort (7), Energy (4)

Velvetian Loveseat

Cost: §1,511

Motives: Comfort (7), Energy (5), Room (4)

Vinyl-Hide Retro Sofa

Cost: §2,349

Motives: Comfort (10), Energy (5), Room (4)

Other
Red Canvas Director's Chair

Cost: §68

Motive: Comfort (2)

Decadent Theater Chairs

Cost: §253

Motive: Comfort (4)

Outdoors Bench

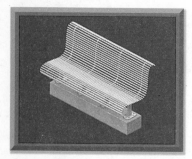

Cost: §275

Motive: Comfort (2)

Surfaces

Counters

White Tile Fantasy Spa Counter

Cost: §299

Motive: —

Neophilic Boutique Counter

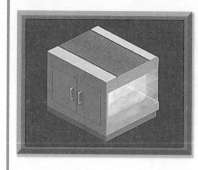

Cost: §767

Motive: —

Tables

Semi-Seedy Lounge Table

Cost: §215

Motive: —

Design by Committee Dining Table

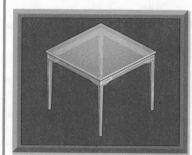

Cost: §289

Motive: Room (1)

...warm Dining Table

Cost: §389

Motive: Room (1)

Neo-Contemporary Modern End Table

Cost: §449

Motive: Room (2)

Tables

...d Roadie's Titanium Tortoise Cases

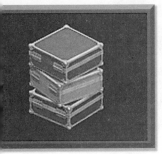

Cost: §60

Motive: —

Other
Cabinet Noir

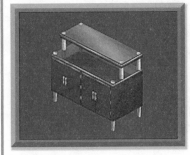

Cost: §2,199

Motive: Room (4)

...orative Wood Block Table

Cost: §189

Motive: Room (1)

Decorative

Paintings
"Measure of Ones and Zeroes" Wall Sculpture

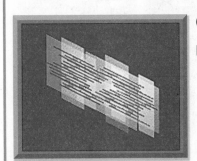

Cost: §850

Motive: Room (3)

"As Scene in Toaster Rockets" Matte Print

Cost: §250

Motive: Room (2)

"The Face of Deco" Canvas Original

Cost: §2,699

Motive: Room (7)

Motivational Pilaster

Cost: §588

Motive: Room (2)

Cascading Corporate Water Wall

Cost: §4,700

Motive: Room (8)

Archetype of Design

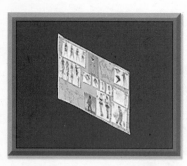

Cost: §900

Motive: Room (3)

The Modern Day Phoenix

Cost: §9,099

Motive: Room (9)

Iptures

ms Fine Dummy

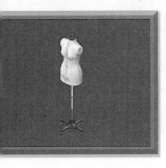

Cost: §65

Motive: Room (1)

Kraken of the Midnight Sea

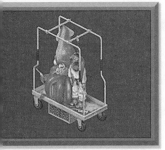

Cost: §169

Motive: Room (1)

ossible Image Design Doll

Cost: §313

Motive: Room (1)

Notes in Motion

Cost: §937

Motive: Room (3)

Sacrifice of the Euphrytian Maidens

Cost: §2,555

Motive: Room (5)

Bronze Likeness of Jerry Martin

Cost: §11,111

Motive: Room (10)

"Knight's War" Statue in Marble

Cost: §16,000

Motive: Room (10)

"The Peace of Fashion" Marble Statue

Cost: §16,019

Motive: Room (10)

Rugs
SimSafari Trophy Rug

Cost: §6,600

Motive: Room (7)

Zythrus Morphos Area Rug

Cost: §11,000

Motive: Room (9)

Plants
Ginormous Potted Palm

Cost: §300

Motive: Room (3)

Other
Sub-Lumen Discretion Awning

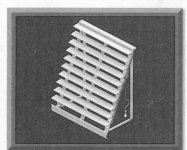

Cost: §65

Motive: Room (1)

...y in Red

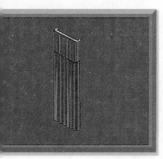

Cost: §139

Motive: —

TrueLife Photographic Camera

Cost: §899

Motive: —

...ngled Ebullience Wall

Cost: §215

Motive: Room (2)

"Over Time" Gold Album

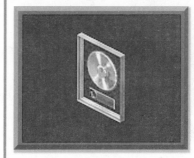

Cost: §3,500

Motive: Room (7)

Stream Accu-Clock

Cost: §335

Motive: Room (2)

Platinum Album Keepsake

Cost: §5,499

Motive: Room (8)

"Epith y Oraia Eleny" in White Marble

Cost: §4,000

Motive: Room (6)

Aqua-Rich-ium

Cost: §4,999

Motive: Room (8)

Petra Pietra Memorial Fountain

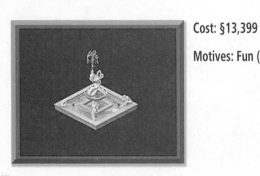

Cost: §13,399

Motives: Fun (2), Room (9)

Electronics

Video

Wall-Mounted TV

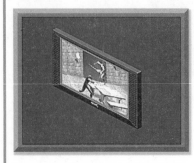

Cost: §7,999

Motives: Fun (8), Room

Notes: Group activity

Audio

Tall Reference 300 Loudspeaker

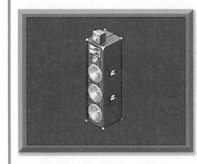

Cost: §229

Motive: Room (2)

Musicphile Giga-Fi Stereo

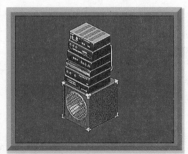

Cost: §1,672

Motives: Fun (5), Room

Notes: Group activity

Digital Satellite

Cost: §3,999

Motive: —

...liances

...e Roger's Culinary Offerings

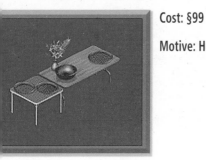

Cost: §99

Motive: Hunger (4)

...mbing

...ts

...t of Gold Replica

Cost: §2,499

Motives: Comfort (2), Bladder (8), Room (4)

Tubs

Jewel in the Crown Spa Tub

Cost: §9,999

Motives: Comfort (7), Hygiene (3), Fun (3)

Notes: Can only be used by adults; group activity

Other

WhisperSteam Personal Steamer

Cost: §2,336

Motives: Comfort (4), Hygiene (5)

Notes: Can only be used by adults

Ponce de Leon Tub

Cost: §4,447

Motives: Comfort (7), Fun (2)

Notes: Can only be used by adults

Lighting

Table Lamps
Light Beside You

Cost: §95

Motive: —

Standing Lamps
Deluge Deflector Light Source

Cost: §365

Motive: —

Lummox Lot #282a

Cost: §429

Motive: Room (1)

Sun Simulator Studio Light

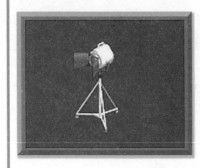

Cost: §485

Motive: —

Barnstormer Studio Light

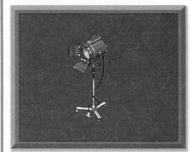

Cost: §535

Motive: —

Wall Lamps
Survivor Outdoor Light

Cost: §25

Motive: —

orld's Stage Exterior Wall Sconce

Cost: §55

Motive: —

Claw of Lummox

Cost: §215

Motive: Room (1)

pia Wall Sconce

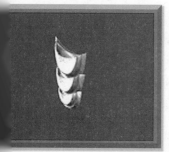

Cost: §265

Motive: Room (1)

#5 Special with Volutes Wall Lamp

Cost: §345

Motive: Room (1)

Hanging Lamps
McLeod's Chandelier of Loneliness

Cost: §629

Motive: Room (4)

Other
Candle Expression in Red

Cost: §35

Motive: —

Miscellaneous

Recreation

Impruv U Pettegrew Massage Table

Cost: §236

Motive: —

Buccaneer's Delight Pool Table

Cost: §6,888

Motives: Fun (7), Room (3)

Notes: Can only be used by adults; group activity

Energize! Oxygen Bar

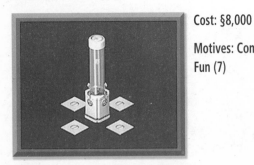

Cost: §8,000

Motives: Comfort (4), Fun (7)

Notes: Can only be used by adults; group activity

Galileo's Free-for-All

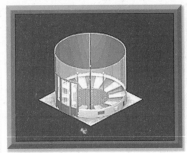

Cost: §16,999

Motive: Fun (10)

Aquatic Playhouse

Cost: §19,999

Motives: Fun (10), Room (4)

Notes: Can only be used by adults

Knowledge

The Face of Shakespeare

Cost: §2,339

Motives: Fun (3), Roo

Notes: + Charisma

tivity

omatic Absolute Sound Keyboard

Cost: §4,481

Motives: Fun (4), Room (5)

: + Creativity; group activity

drobe

or to the World

Cost: §399

Motive: Room (1)

: + Charisma; can only be used by adults

ing Dresser

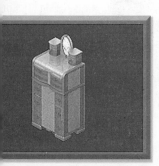

Cost: §2,049

Motive: Room (3)

Blue Steel Dresser

Cost: §3,099

Motive: Room (5)

Other

The Machine Workout Bench

Cost: §2,099

Motive: Room (2)

Notes: + Body; can only be used by adults

The Genius Loci Karaoke Stage

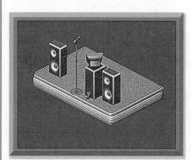

Cost: §4,413

Motive: Fun (6)

Notes: Group activity

Build Mode

Wall and Fence Tool

Neighbor Begone Privacy Fence

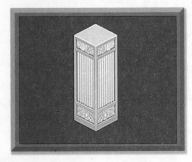

Cost: §175

Motive: —

Arch a la Deco

Cost: §260

Motive: —

Studio Fence

Cost: §299

Motive: —

Neo-Classic Infusion Column

Cost: §349

Motive: —

Wallpaper Tool

"High Fashion in Glass" Wall Paneling

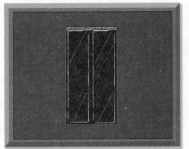

Cost: §3

Motive: —

"Inert States" Wall Paneling

Cost: §3

Motive: —

rile Style" Wall Treatment

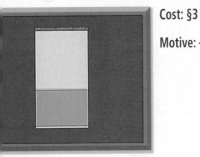

Cost: §3

Motive: —

e" Wallpaper

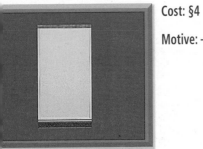

Cost: §4

Motive: —

rm Welcome" Wall Treatment

Cost: §4

Motive: —

Blue Screen Background

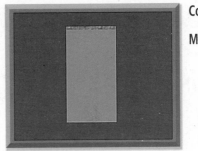

Cost: §4

Motive: —

Green Screen Background

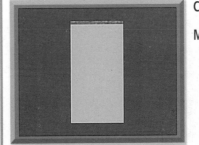

Cost: §4

Motive: —

"Darkest Irony" Wall Motif

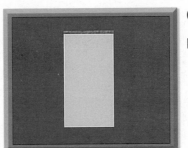

Cost: §5

Motive: —

"Movie Mania" Wall Treatment

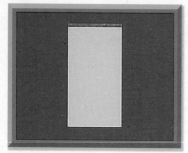

Cost: §5

Motive: —

"The Fanciful Stone" Paneling

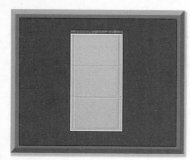

Cost: §5

Motive: —

"Ornamental Strips on Cream" Wall

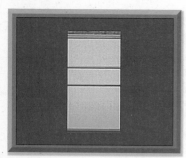

Cost: §6

Motive: —

"Raw Function" Wall

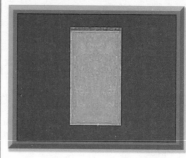

Cost: §6

Motive: —

"Studio 237" Wall Treatment

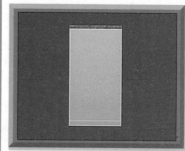

Cost: §6

Motive: —

Stone Treatment #43

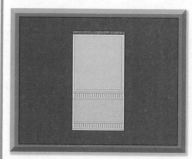

Cost: §6

Motive: —

...ancholy Paint

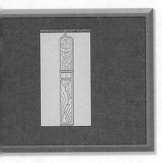

Cost: §7

Motive: —

...Smooth Bricks

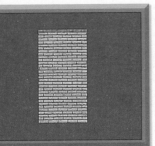

Cost: §7

Motive: —

...ank Canvas" Tent

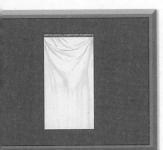

Cost: §8

Motive: —

Carpet Wall

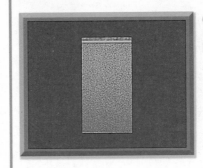

Cost: §8

Motive: —

"The Paradigm" Wallpaper

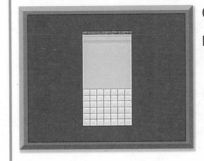

Cost: §9

Motive: —

DeLuxe Gold Fleck Tile

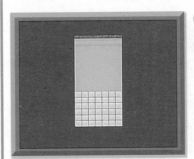

Cost: §9

Motive: —

Sterilized White Tile

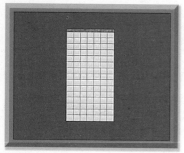

Cost: §9

Motive: —

Sound-Proofing Wall Panel

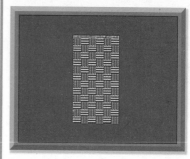

Cost: §11

Motive: —

Quiet Room Wall Treatment

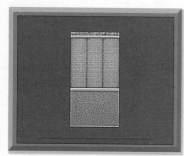

Cost: §10

Motive: —

"Expressions in Brick" Wall Treatment

Cost: §12

Motive: —

"Stacked Rock" Wall

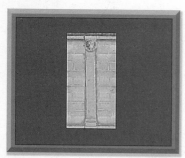

Cost: §11

Motive: —

"Unknowable" Brick Wall

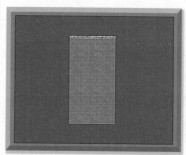

Cost: §12

Motive: —

k Paint

Cost: §12

Motive: —

Red Velvet Wall Treatment

Cost: §14

Motive: —

rbleous" Wall Treatment

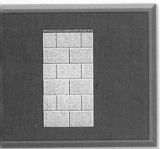

Cost: §13

Motive: —

Authentic Castle Wall

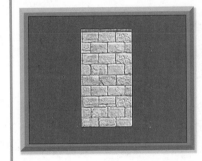

Cost: §15

Motive: —

ony Front" Wall Treatment

Cost: §13

Motive: —

Stair Tool
Social Climber Stairs

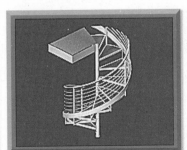

Cost: §3,799

Motive: —

Plant Tool
Hedge Topiary Sectional

Cost: §190

Motive: —

"Simply Carpet" Tile

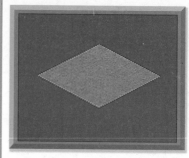

Cost: §4

Motive: —

Citrus sinensis

Cost: §310

Motive: —

Blue Screen Tile

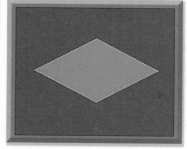

Cost: §4

Motive: —

Floor Tool
"Cellulistic" Carpet

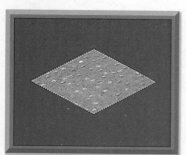

Cost: §3

Motive: —

Green Screen Tile

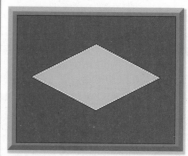

Cost: §4

Motive: —

...ther's Dream" Carpet

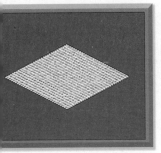

Cost: §5

Motive: —

Decorative Pattern b22 Tile

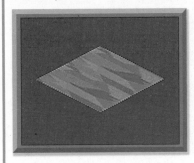

Cost: §6

Motive: —

...rkhorse" Black Linoleum

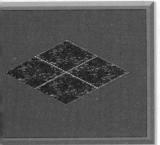

Cost: §5

Motive: —

Decorative Pattern a22 Tile

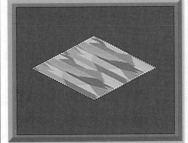

Cost: §6

Motive: —

...listic Grate Prop

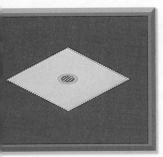

Cost: §6

Motive: —

"Platinum" Carpet

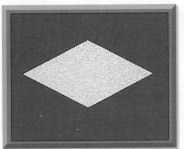

Cost: §6

Motive: —

"Ostentation" Carpet

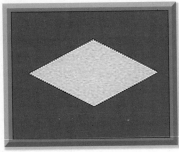

Cost: §6

Motive: —

Audio Absorbing Floor Treatment

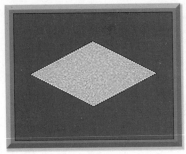

Cost: §7

Motive: —

"Blue Sky" Ceramic Tile

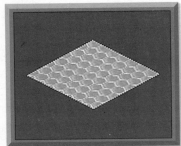

Cost: §7

Motive: —

"Royal Red" Carpet

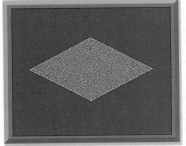

Cost: §8

Motive: —

"Plain" White Tile

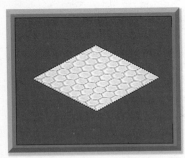

Cost: §7

Motive: —

"Purple Obsession" Carpet

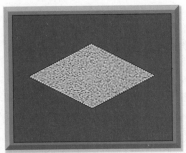

Cost: §8

Motive: —

vanced Ode to Geometry" Tile

Cost: §9

Motive: —

Designer Core-Polished Corundum

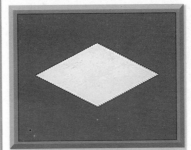

Cost: §9

Motive: —

mented Shaped" Concrete

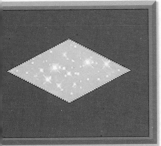

Cost: §9

Motive: —

Gray Tile

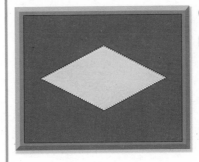

Cost: §9

Motive: —

le to Geometry" Tile

Cost: §9

Motive: —

Generic Concrete

Cost: §10

Motive: —

"Tsang's Navy" Carpet

Cost: §10

Motive: —

PermaStone Tumbled Paver

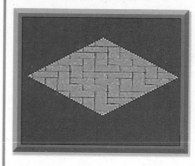

Cost: §11

Motive: —

"Crimsomnia" Carpet

Cost: §10

Motive: —

"Starry" Tile

Cost: §12

Motive: —

"Collage" Ceramic Tile

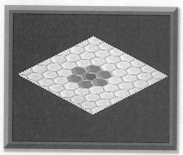

Cost: §10

Motive: —

Sanitary Linoleum

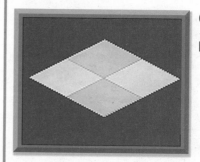

Cost: §13

Motive: —

...piration" Tile

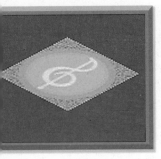

Cost: §13

Motive: —

...naissance Smoothed Stone

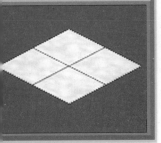

Cost: §15

Motive: —

...lieval Earthen Stone

Cost: §15

Motive: —

"Organic" Wood Tile

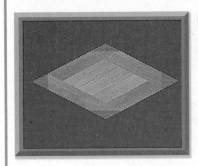

Cost: §15

Motive: —

'06 Mosaic

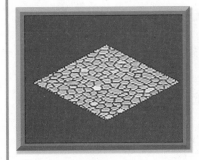

Cost: §17

Motive: —

Classic Cobblestone

Cost: §21

Motive: —

"The Cobbled Star" Tile

Cost: §22

Motive: —

Factitious Glass Door

Cost: §277

Motive: —

Door Tool

Zeddy-Lock Celebrity Security Door

Cost: §139

Motive: —

Notes: Restricts entrance to Sims with at least two stars

Doorless Arch

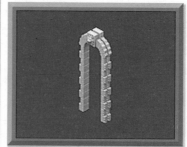

Cost: §349

Motive: —

Simply Modern Door

Cost: §173

Motive: —

M&S Eulogy Door

Cost: §381

Motive: —

h-Spring Public Door

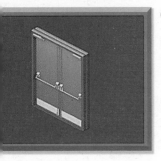

Cost: §399

Motive: —

tive Cycloid Door

Cost: §522

Motive: —

s Lithos Tone Archway

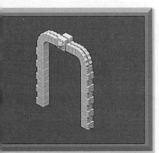

Cost: §599

Motive: —

Grand Entrance Double Door

Cost: §699

Motive: —

Windows

Barbizon Cascade Window

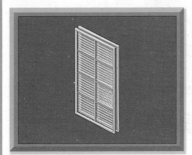

Cost: §73

Motive: —

Window en Zen

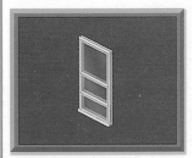

Cost: §115

Motive: —

Dichotomizer Window

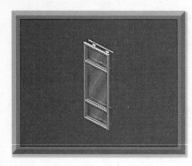

Cost: §160

Motive: —

Solid Glass Window

Cost: §335

Motive: —

Designer Window

Cost: §500

Motive: —

Studio Town Only

Food

Decorative

"Two Men, a Woman, and One Monkey" Poster

Cost: §35

Motive: —

Sunday Night Fashion Match-up

Cost: §69

Motive: Room (1)

Blue Inca Pilot Live! Poster

Cost: §111

Motive: Room (1)

y Yeti Attacks! Movie Poster

Cost: §159

Motive: Room (1)

ronics

rn of the Vacuum Tube

Cost: §499

Motive: —

iances

ally Perfect Smoothie Stand

Cost: §4,888

Motive: Hunger (3)

: Can only be used by adults

Sushi Yatai

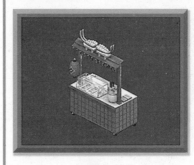

Cost: §6,714

Motive: Hunger (5)

Notes: Can only be used by adults

Shops

Electronics

Electronic Estimator Cash Register

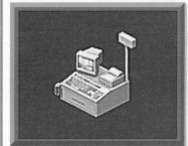

Cost: §289

Motive: —

Miscellaneous

Geometric Joy Waste Cube

Cost: §379

Motive: —

Luxury Dressing Booth by Posh

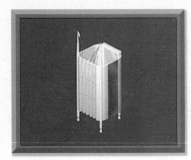

Cost: §699

Motive: —

Savoir Faire Poster Display

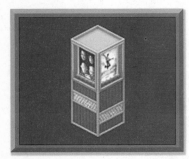

Cost: §1,112

Motive: —

Bob's Haute Couture Rack

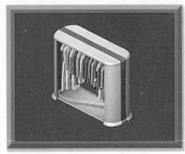

Cost: §6,999

Motive: —

Studio

Decorative

Digital Television Camera

Cost: §1,549

Motive: —

m FOV Studio Camera

Cost: §2,229

Motive: —

The Flawless Photo Shoot

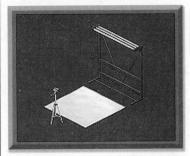

Cost: §5,999

Motive: —

Notes: Can only be used by adults

cellaneous

nt Potentiometer Open Mic Stage

Cost: §1,015

Motive: —

s: Can only be used by adults; group activity

ActionWorks Television Studio Hospital Set

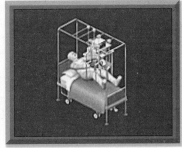

Cost: §8,999

Motive: —

Notes: Can only be used by adults

Mini Trailer for the Stars

Cost: §10,000

Motives: Comfort (5), Bladder (6), Fun (3)

Notes: Can only be used by adults

Cacophonator 16R5 Sound Enhancement Booth

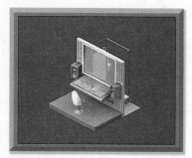

Cost: §12,999

Motive: —

Notes: Can only be used by adults

The Walk of Fame

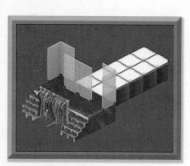

Cost: §17,999

Motive: —

Notes: Can only be used by adults

The Music Video Generation Stage

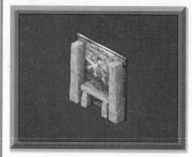

Cost: §21,999

Motive: —

Notes: Can only be used by adults

Director's Turf Sound Stage

Cost: §24,999

Motive: —

Notes: Can only be used by adults

CHAPTER 15: INTERACTION TABLES

Introduction

The following tables contain relevant data for every interaction in *The Sims Superstar*, including Short Term and Long Term Relationships. The interactions are broken down into four sections: adult to adult, adult to child, child to adult, and child to child. Each section contains three tables. The first table describes the general requirements for a successful interaction, and the second lists the effects of all possible results of each interaction. The third lists the conditions that determine whether or not a specific interaction shows up as an option in your menus. Use these tables to gauge your chance of success with each interaction.

Adult-to-Adult Interactions

Key	
>	Greater than
≥	Greater than or equal to
<	Less than
≤	Less than or equal to

Adult Interaction Success Requirements

CATEGORY	INTERACTION	INITIATOR REQUIREMENTS	RECIPIENT REQUIREMENTS
Ask	How Are You?	None	Mood ≥ -80
	How's Work?	None	Mood ≥ -30
	Invite Downtown	None	Energy ≥ 0, Daily ≥ -20
	Invite Home	None	Mood ≥ 40, Outgoing > 9
		None	Mood ≥ 40, Lifetime > 50
		None	Mood ≥ 40, Daily ≥ 55, Outgoing > 5
		None	Mood ≥ 40, Daily ≥ 70
	Let's Hang Out/Date	Hygiene > -10	Daily > 10
	Move In	None	Lifetime ≥ 60, Mood ≥ 45, Daily ≥ 85
	Propose	Different Genders	Love, Lifetime > 80, Daily > 75, Mood > 6
	What Are You Into?	None	Mood ≥ -30
Attack	Fight	Body ≥ Recipient's Body	None
	Shove	Body ≥ Recipient's Body +2	None
	Slap	Body > Recipient's Body	None
	Slap Fight	None	Daily ≥ 20, Mood ≥ 10, Playful ≥ 6
Brag	Boast	None	Daily between 0 and 25, Mood > 10
	Flex	None	Nice ≥ 9
		Body > Recipient's Body +5	None
		None	Daily ≥ 30
		None	Mood ≥ 25
	Primp	None	Daily ≥ 50
		None	Daily > 0, Outgoing > 6
		None	Daily > 0, Mood ≥ 35

Adult Interaction Success Requirements, continued

CATEGORY	INTERACTION	INITIATOR REQUIREMENTS	RECIPIENT REQUIREMENTS
Cheer Up	Comfort	None	Daily ≥ 65
		None	Daily > 55, Outgoing ≤ 3
	Encourage	None	Outgoing > 7
		None	Mood ≥ -25
	With Puppet	None	Playful > 7
		None	Nice ≥ 4, Mood ≥ -30
		None	Nice < 4, Mood ≥ -40
Compliment	Admire	None	Nice ≤ 3, Mood > 60
		None	Nice > 3, Daily > -25
		None	Nice > 3, Mood > 10
	Worship	None	Daily ≥ 20, Charisma ≥ 7
		None	Daily ≥ 20, Outgoing ≤ 3, Mood > 60
		None	Daily ≥ 20, Outgoing > 3, Nice > 4
		None	Daily ≥ 20, Outgoing > 3, Nice ≤ 3, Mood > 60
Dance	Lively	None	Daily > -10, Energy ≥ 10, Mood ≥ 0, Outgoing > 3
		None	Daily > -10, Energy ≥ 10, Mood ≥ 0, Outgoing ≤ 3, Mood > 40
		None	Daily > -10, Energy ≥ 10, Mood ≥ 0, Outgoing ≤ 3, Daily > 30
	Slow	Hygiene > 20	Energy > 10, Mood > 20, Daily > -10, Outgoing > 3
		Hygiene > 20	Energy > 10, Mood > 20, Daily > -10, Lifetime ≥ 35
		Hygiene > 20	Energy > 10, Mood > 40, Outgoing ≤ 3
		Hygiene > 20	Energy > 10, Mood > 20, Daily > 30, Lifetime ≥ 35

Adult Interaction Success Requirements, continued

CATEGORY	INTERACTION	INITIATOR REQUIREMENTS	RECIPIENT REQUIREMENTS
Entertain	Joke	None	Playful > 7
		None	Playful < 3, Daily > 30
		None	Playful ≥ 3, Mood > 50, Daily > 30
	(Mild Accept)	None	Playful ≥ 3, Daily < -10
	(Mild Accept)	None	Playful < 3, Mood > 50, Daily < -10
	Juggle	None	Playful > 7
		None	Playful ≥ 3, Daily > 20
		None	Playful < 3, Mood > 50, Daily > 20
	With Puppet	None	Nice < 4, Mood > 50
		None	Nice ≥ 3, Playful ≥ 7
		None	Nice ≥ 3, Playful < 3, Mood > 50
Flirt	Check Out	None	Mood ≥ -10, Outgoing ≥ 7
		None	Mood ≥ -10, Outgoing > 2, Mood > 40
		None	Mood ≥ -10, Outgoing > 2, Daily > 20
		None	Mood ≥ -10, Outgoing ≤ 2, Charisma ≥ 3
		None	Mood ≥ -10, Outgoing ≤ 2, Body ≥ 5
		None	Mood ≥ -10, Outgoing ≤ 2, Mood > 30
		None	Mood ≥ -10, Outgoing ≤ 2, Daily > 15
	Growl	None	Mood ≥ 20, Outgoing ≥ 9
		None	Mood < 20, Lifetime ≥ 30
		None	Outgoing ≥ 4
		None	Mood > 50
		None	Daily > 25
	Back Rub	None	Mood > 20, Daily or Lifetime > 35
		None	Mood > 20, Outgoing ≥ 6
		None	Mood > 20, Daily > 30
	Sweet Talk	None	Daily or Lifetime ≥ 40
Greet	Wave	None	Lifetime > -40
	Shake Hands	None	Lifetime ≥ -20
	Air Kiss	None	Lifetime ≥ 20
	Kiss Cheek	None	Lifetime ≥ 20
	Hug	None	Lifetime > -20
	Romantic Kiss	None	Lifetime ≥ 50
		In Love	In Love
	Suave Kiss	None	Lifetime > 15

...ult Interaction Success Requirements, continued

CATEGORY	INTERACTION	INITIATOR REQUIREMENTS	RECIPIENT REQUIREMENTS
Hug	Friendly	Hygiene ≥ -40	Mood > 50
		Hygiene ≥ -40	Daily > 30
		Hygiene ≥ -40	Nice ≥ 2, Mood > 10
	Intimate	Hygiene ≥ -40	Nice ≥ 3, Daily > 20
		Hygiene ≥ -40	Nice < 3, Mood > 60
		Hygiene ≥ -40	Nice < 3, Daily or Lifetime > 30
	Leap into Arms	Hygiene ≥ -40	Nice or Playful ≥ 7
		Hygiene ≥ -40	Mood > 40
		Hygiene ≥ -40	Daily > 45
		Hygiene ≥ -40	Lifetime > 30
	Romantic	Hygiene ≥ -40	Nice < 3, Mood > 60
		Hygiene ≥ -40	Nice < 3, Daily > 50
		Hygiene ≥ -40	Nice < 3, Lifetime > 40
		Hygiene ≥ -40	Nice ≥ 3, Daily > 30
		Hygiene ≥ -40	Nice ≥ 3, Lifetime > 35
Insult	Shake Fist	None	Nice ≥ 4, -30 < Mood < 0
		None	Nice ≥ 4, Mood > 0, Daily ≤ 20
	Poke	None	Nice < 4
		None	Nice ≥ 4, Mood ≤ 0
		None	Nice ≥ 4, Mood > 0, Daily < 20
Kiss	Peck	None	Mood > 0, Lifetime ≥ 10, Daily ≥ 20
		None	Mood > 0, Daily ≥ 20
	Polite	None	Daily ≥ 20, Lifetime > 10, Mood ≥ 25
	Suave	None	Mood >0, Lifetime ≥ 15, Daily ≥ 30
	Romantic	None	Crush
		None	Daily > 60, Mood > 40
		None	Lifetime > 60
	Passionate	None	Lifetime > 40, Daily ≥ 50, Mood ≥ 30
	Deep Kiss	None	Love, Mood ≥ 40
...ag	About Friends	None	Mood > 40
		None	Mood ≥ 0, Nice ≥ 7
	About House	None	Mood > 40
		None	Mood ≥ 0, Nice ≥ 7
	About Money	None	Mood > 40
		None	Mood ≥ 0, Nice ≥ 7

Adult Interaction Success Requirements, continued

CATEGORY	INTERACTION	INITIATOR REQUIREMENTS	RECIPIENT REQUIREMENTS
Plead	Apologize	None	Mood > -5
		None	Lifetime ≥ 25
	Grovel	None	Mood ≥ -15
		None	Lifetime ≥ 25
Say Good-bye	Shoo	None	Daily ≤ 10
	Shake Hands	None	Daily ≥ 20
		None	Lifetime ≥ 10
	Wave	None	Daily or Lifetime ≤ 20
	Kiss Cheek	None	Daily ≥ 20
		None	Lifetime ≥ 30
	Hug	None	Daily or Lifetime ≥ 30
	Kiss Hand	None	Nice ≤ 3, Daily ≥ 60
		None	Nice ≤ 3, Lifetime ≥ 50
		None	Nice > 3, Daily or Lifetime ≥ 40
	Polite Kiss	None	Outgoing ≥ 6, Daily ≥ 40
		None	Outgoing ≥ 6, Lifetime ≥ 60
		None	Outgoing < 6, Daily or Lifetime ≥ 60
	Passionate Kiss	None	Outgoing ≥ 7, Daily ≥ 60
		None	Outgoing ≥ 7, Lifetime ≥ 65
		None	Outgoing < 7, Daily ≥ 80
		None	Outgoing < 7, Lifetime ≥ 65
Talk	About Interests	(Always Accepted)	None
	Change Subject	(Always Accepted)	None
	Gossip	None	Daily > 40
Tease	Imitate	None	Playful > 6, Mood > 50
		None	Playful > 6, Mood < 0
		None	Daily ≥ -15, Lifetime > 50, Playful ≤ 6
	Taunt	None	Mood or Daily > -20
	Raspberry	None	Mood or Daily ≥ -20, Lifetime > 25
	Scare	None	Playful ≥ 5
		None	Mood > 25
Tickle	Ribs	None	Playful > 5
		None	Mood > 50
	Extreme	None	Playful > 5
		None	Mood > 50

lt Social Interaction Results

TERACTION	RESPONSE	DAILY RELATIONSHIP CHANGE	LIFETIME RELATIONSHIP CHANGE	SOCIAL SCORE CHANGE
TTACKS				
ap	Cry	0	0	3
	Slap Back	-10	-3	-7
e Slapped	Cry	-20	-10	-17
	Slap Back	-15	-7	3
ssy Fight	Cry	0	0	3
	Fight Back	-8	-2	-5
e Sissy Fought	Cry	-16	-8	-13
	Fight Back	-13	-5	3
ove	Cry	0	0	3
	Shove Back	-8	-2	-5
e Shoved	Cry	-16	-8	-13
	Shove Back	-13	-5	3
RAGGING				
ag	Good	5	0	10
	Bad	-5	0	0
e Bragged To	Good	3	0	5
	Bad	-5	0	0
NSULTS				
sult	Cry	-6	-3	0
	Stoic	0	-1	3
	Angry	-10	-1	5
e Insulted	Cry	-12	-5	-10
	Stoic	-8	0	-5
	Angry	-14	-2	-7
EASING				
aunt	Giggle	4	0	7
	Cry	0	0	3
e Taunted	Giggle	4	0	7
	Cry	-10	0	-7

Adult Social Interaction Results, continued

INTERACTION	RESPONSE	DAILY RELATIONSHIP CHANGE	LIFETIME RELATIONSHIP CHANGE	SOCIAL SCORE CHANGE
Imitate with Puppet	Giggle	4	0	7
	Cry	0	0	3
Be Imitated with Puppet	Giggle	4	0	7
	Cry	-10	0	-7
Scare	Laugh	5	0	10
	Angry	-5	0	0
Be Scared	Laugh	5	0	8
	Angry	-10	0	0
TICKLING				
Tickle	Laugh	8	0	10
	Refuse	-5	-1	0
Be Tickled	Laugh	5	0	10
	Refuse	-8	-2	0
Extreme Tickle	Laugh	8	0	10
	Refuse	-5	-1	0
Be Extreme Tickled	Laugh	5	0	10
	Refuse	-5	-1	0
CHEERING				
Motivate	Good	5	0	7
	Mild	0	0	5
	Bad	-3	0	0
Be Motivated	Good	10	0	10
	Mild	0	0	5
	Bad	-10	0	0
Cheer Up with Puppet	Good	5	0	7 (Sensitive: 6
	Mild	0	0	5
	Bad	-3	0	0
Be Cheered Up with Puppet	Good	6	0	10
	Mild	0	0	5
	Bad	-10	0	0

Adult Social Interaction Results, continued

INTERACTION	RESPONSE	DAILY RELATIONSHIP CHANGE	LIFETIME RELATIONSHIP CHANGE	SOCIAL SCORE CHANGE
COMPLIMENTS				
Admire	Accept	4	1	5
	Reject	-10	-1	0
Be Admired	Accept	3	2	11
	Reject	-7	-2	0
Worship	Accept	3	1	5
	Reject	-15	-5	0
Be Worshiped	Accept	4	2	15
	Reject	-10	-4	0
DANCING				
Dance Lively	Accept	6	0	13
	Reject	-5	0	0
Be Danced with Lively	Accept	6	0	13
	Reject	-5	0	0
Dance Slow	Accept	8	2	15
	Reject	-10	-3	-4
Be Danced with Slowly	Accept	8	2	15
	Reject	-7	-2	0
ENTERTAINING				
Joke	Laugh	3	0	9
	Giggle	2	0	7
	Fail	-6	0	0
Hear Joke	Laugh	4	0	10
	Giggle	3	0	7
	Fail	-7	0	0
Juggle or Puppet	Laugh	3	0	7
	Fail	-10	0	0
Watch Juggle	Laugh	4	0	10
	Fail	-7	0	0
Watch Puppet	Laugh	4	0	13
	Fail	-7	0	0

Adult Social Interaction Results, continued

INTERACTION	RESPONSE	DAILY RELATIONSHIP CHANGE	LIFETIME RELATIONSHIP CHANGE	SOCIAL SCORE CHANG
FLIRTATION				
Give Backrub	Accept	3	2	7
	Reject	-7	-2	0
Receive Backrub	Accept	5	3	10
	Reject	-10	-3	0
Give Suggestion	Accept	4	1	10
	Ignore	-5	0	0
	Reject	-5	-1	-10
Receive Suggestion	Accept	6	1	10
	Ignore	-3	0	0
	Reject	-7	-2	0
Check Out	Accept	5	2	10
	Ignore	-5	0	0
	Reject	-8	-1	-10
Be Checked Out	Accept	5	2	10
	Ignore	-3	0	0
	Reject	-10	-3	0
Growl	Accept	5	2	10
	Ignore	-5	0	0
	Reject	-8	-2	-10
Receive Growl	Accept	6	2	10
	Ignore	-3	0	0
	Reject	-10	-3	0
GOOD-BYES				
Shake Hand	Good	2	0	0
	Bad	-2	0	0
Have Hand Shaken	Good	2	0	0
	Bad	-2	0	0
Hug	Good	5	0	0
	Bad	-5	0	0
Be Hugged	Good	5	0	0
	Bad	-5	0	0

Social Interaction Results, continued

INTERACTION	RESPONSE	DAILY RELATIONSHIP CHANGE	LIFETIME RELATIONSHIP CHANGE	SOCIAL SCORE CHANGE
lite Kiss	Good	7	2	0
	Bad	-7	-3	0
Politely Kissed	Good	7	3	0
	Bad	-7	-2	0
ss Cheek	Good	3	0	0
	Bad	-3	0	0
ve Cheek Kissed	Good	3	0	0
	Bad	-3	0	0
ss Hand	Good	3	1	0
	Bad	-3	-3	0
ve Hand Kissed	Good	3	2	0
	Bad	-3	-2	0
ssionate Kiss	Good	10	5	0
	Bad	-10	-6	0
Passionately Kissed	Good	10	5	0
	Bad	-10	-6	0
ave	Good	1	0	0
	Bad	-1	0	0
Waved To	Good	1	0	0
	Bad	-1	0	0
oo	Good	1	0	0
	Neutral	0	0	0
	Bad	0	0	0
Shooed	Good	1	0	0
	Neutral	0	0	0
	Bad	-3	0	0
REETINGS				
ave	Good	1	0	2
	Bad	–2	0	2
ake Hand	Good	1	0	2
	Bad	-2	-2	0

Adult Social Interaction Results, continued

INTERACTION	RESPONSE	DAILY RELATIONSHIP CHANGE	LIFETIME RELATIONSHIP CHANGE	SOCIAL SCORE CHANGE
Have Hand Shaken	Good	2	1	0
	Bad	-2	-2	0
Air Kiss	Good	2	0	3
	Bad	-4	0	-3
Be Air Kissed	Good	2	0	3
	Bad	-4	0	-3
Polite Kiss	Good	5	1	5
	Bad	-8	-2	-4
Be Politely Kissed	Good	5	5	1
	Bad	-6	-1	-3
Kiss Hand	Good	5	1	5
	Bad	-6	-2	-5
Have Hand Kissed	Good	5	1	10
	Bad	-6	-1	-3
Hug	Good	8	2	8
	Bad	-8	-2	-4
Be Hugged	Good	8	2	8
	Bad	-8	-1	-3
Romantic Kiss	Good	12	3	12
	Bad	-12	-2	-5
Be Romantically Kissed	Good	12	3	12
	Bad	-12	-2	-3

HUGS

INTERACTION	RESPONSE	DAILY RELATIONSHIP CHANGE	LIFETIME RELATIONSHIP CHANGE	SOCIAL SCORE CHANGE
Friendly Hug	Accept	4	1	8
	Tentative	2	0	5
	Refuse	-5	-1	0
Receive Friendly Hug	Accept	5	1	8
	Tentative	4	0	5
	Refuse	-5	-1	0
Body Hug	Accept	5	2	10
	Tentative	5	0	7
	Refuse	-10	-3	0

ERACTION	RESPONSE	DAILY RELATIONSHIP CHANGE	LIFETIME RELATIONSHIP CHANGE	SOCIAL SCORE CHANGE
Body Hugged	Accept	8	2	10
	Tentative	4	0	7
	Refuse	-10	-2	0
mantic Hug	Accept	5	2	10
	Tentative	5	0	7
	Reject	-10	-3	0
Romantically Hugged	Accept	8	2	10
	Tentative	4	0	7
	Reject	-10	-2	0
ing Hug	Accept	9	2	10
	Refuse	-15	-4	0
ceive Flying Hug	Accept	8	2	10
	Tentative	4	0	7
	Refuse	-10	-2	0

SSES

s Hand	Passionate	5	0	5
	Polite	4	0	4
	Deny	-5	-1	4
ve Hand Kissed	Passionate	5	0	5
	Polite	4	0	4
	Deny	-5	0	0
ss Polite	Passionate	6	1	7
	Polite	5	0	5
	Deny	-7	-1	4
Kissed Politely	Passionate	6	1	7
	Polite	5	0	5
	Deny	-6	-1	0
s Tentatively	Passionate	8	2	8
	Polite	6	1	6
	Deny	-9	-2	4

Adult Social Interaction Results, continued

INTERACTION	RESPONSE	DAILY RELATIONSHIP CHANGE	LIFETIME RELATIONSHIP CHANGE	SOCIAL SCORE CHANGE
Be Kissed Tentatively	Passionate	8	2	8
	Polite	6	1	6
	Deny	-8	-2	0
Kiss Passionately	Passionate	13	4	10
	Polite	8	2	8
	Deny	-10	-3	4
Be Kissed Passionately	Passionate	13	3	10
	Polite	8	2	8
	Deny	-10	-4	0
Dip Kiss	Passionate	15	5	15
	Polite	10	2	10
	Deny	-15	-5	4
Be Dip Kissed	Passionate	15	5	15
	Polite	10	2	10
	Deny	-15	-5	0
NAGGING				
Nag	Giggle	-1	0	3
	Cry	-4	-1	3
Be Nagged	Giggle	-3	0	4
	Cry	-8	-2	-5
PLEADING				
Apologize	Accept	8	0	8
	Reject	-8	0	3
Be Apologized To	Accept	8	0	8
	Reject	-5	0	3
Grovel	Accept	12	0	8
	Reject	-12	0	3
Be Groveled To	Accept	12	0	8
	Reject	-5	0	3

...lt Interaction Menu Triggers

...TEGORY	INTERACTION	RELATIONSHIP REQUIREMENTS	DISPOSITION REQUIREMENTS
...sk	How Are You?	Daily > -80	Mood > -70
	How's Work?	Daily between –5 and 35, Lifetime < 40	Mood > 0
	Invite Downtown	None	At Home Only
	Invite Home	Daily > 55	Downtown Only
	Let's Hang Out/Date	None	Always Available Downtown
	Move In	Lifetime > 50, Daily > 50	Same Gender
	Propose	Daily > 75	Different Genders, In Love
	What Are You Into?	Daily between –5 and 35, Lifetime < 40	Mood > 0
...ttack	Fight	Daily < -40, Lifetime < 0	Mood < 0
	Shove	Lifetime ≤ 30, Daily < -40	Mood < 0
	Slap	Lifetime ≤ 30, Daily < -40	Mood < 0
	Slapfight	Daily < -40	Playful ≥ 7, Mood < 0
...rag	Boast	None	Daily < 50, Lifetime < 40
	Flex	Daily < 50, Lifetime < 40	Body ≥ 4
	Primp	Daily < 50, Lifetime < 40	Charisma ≥ 2
...heer Up	Comfort	Lifetime > 25, Friends	Outgoing > 3, Mood > 25, Subject's Mood < 0
		Lifetime > 5, Friends	Outgoing ≤ 3, Mood > 20, Subject's Mood < 0
	Encourage	Lifetime > 25, Friends	Charisma ≥ 2, Mood > 25
	With Puppet	Friends	Playful ≥ 6, Outgoing ≥ 4, Mood > 25, Subject's Mood < 0
...ompliment	Admire	Daily between -10 and 40	Mood > 20
	Worship	Daily between -10 and 40, Lifetime between 20 and 80,	Nice > 3, Outgoing > 3 Mood > 20
...ance	Lively	Daily > 30, Lifetime > -25	Energy > 20, Mood > -20, Outgoing > 3
	Slow	Lifetime > 20	Energy > 10

Adult Interaction Menu Triggers, continued

CATEGORY	INTERACTION	RELATIONSHIP REQUIREMENTS	DISPOSITION REQUIREMENTS
Entertain	Joke	Daily > 0, Lifetime between –25 and 70	Playful ≥3, Mood > -10
	Juggle	Daily > -25, Lifetime between 0 and 70	Outgoing > 3, Playful > 4 Mood > 0
	With Puppet	Daily > -25, Lifetime between 0 and 70	Outgoing > 3, Playful > 3 Mood > 0
Flirt	Check Out	Lifetime between –10 and 10, Daily between 5 and 60	Mood > -20
	Growl	Lifetime between –10 and 10, Daily between 5 and 60	Mood > -20
	Backrub	Daily between 30 and 60, Lifetime > 30	Mood > 30
	Sweet Talk	Daily between 25 and 60, Lifetime > -50	Outgoing ≥ 7, Mood > 30
		Daily between 40 and 60, Lifetime > -50	Outgoing < 7, Mood > 30
Greet	Wave	Always Available	
	Shake Hands	Always Available	
	Air Kiss	Lifetime ≥ 5	None
	Kiss Cheek	Lifetime ≥ 20	None
	Hug	Crush	None
	Romantic Kiss	Crush	None
	Suave Kiss	Lifetime > 15	Outgoing ≥ 3
Hug	Friendly	Lifetime > 0, Daily > 15	Mood > 10
	Intimate	Lifetime > 10, Daily > 15	Mood > 20
	Leap into Arms	Daily > 40, Lifetime > 30	Mood > 25, Outgoing > 5
	Romantic	Daily > 40, Lifetime > 40	Mood > 35, Outgoing > 3
Insult	Shake Fist	Lifetime < 50	Nice ≤ 3
		None	Mood < 0
	Poke	Lifetime < 50	Nice < 3
		None	Mood ≤ 0
Kiss	Peck	Daily ≥ 20, Lifetime > 0	Mood > 0
	Polite	Daily ≥ 35, Lifetime > 15	Mood > 15
	Suave	Daily ≥ 25, Lifetime > 10	Mood > 0
	Romantic	Daily ≥ 55, Lifetime > 25	Mood > 25
	Passionate	Daily ≥ 45, Lifetime > 25	Mood > 15
	Deep Kiss	Love	Mood > 25

Interaction Menu Triggers, continued

CATEGORY	INTERACTION	RELATIONSHIP REQUIREMENTS	DISPOSITION REQUIREMENTS
g	About Friends	Lifetime > 40	Mood ≤ -30
	About House	Lifetime > 40	Mood ≤ -30
	About Money	Lifetime > 40	Mood ≤ -3, Cash < §1,000
ad	Apologize	Daily ≤ -10 Lifetime > 5	Mood ≤ -20
	Grovel	Daily > -20, Lifetime > 10	Mood ≤ -40
y Good-bye	Shoo	Daily < -50	None
	Shake Hands	Daily > -50	None
	Wave	Daily > -50	None
	Kiss Cheek	Daily > -10	None
	Hug	Daily > 0	None
	Kiss Hand	Daily > 20	None
	Polite Kiss	Daily ≥ 20	None
	Passionate Kiss	Daily > 20	Outgoing ≥ 7
		Daily > 40	Outgoing < 7
k	About Interests	None	Available in Ongoing Conversation
	Change Subject	None	Available in Ongoing Conversation
	Gossip	None	Mood > -25
ase	Imitate	None	Playful > 5, Mood < 15
		Daily < -20	Playful > 5, Nice < 5
	Taunt	None	Mood < 30, Nice < 5
		Daily < -20	Nice < 5
	Raspberry	None	Mood < 15, Nice < 5
		Daily < -20	Nice < 5
	Scare	None	Playful ≥ 5, Mood < 30, Nice < 5
kle	Ribs	Daily > 10	Playful ≥4, Nice > 4
	Extreme	Daily > 10, Lifetime between 20 and 70	Playful > 3, Nice > 4

Adult-to-Child Interactions

Adult-to-Child Interaction Success Requirements

CATEGORY	INTERACTION	RECIPIENT REQUIREMENTS
Brag		Mood > 50, Daily > 50
Cheer Up		Social ≤ 0
		Daily ≥ 0
Entertain	Joke	Playful ≥ 2
		Mood ≥ 30
	Juggle	Playful ≥ 2
		Mood ≥ 30
Hug	Nice	Mood ≥ 20
		Daily ≥ 10
	Friendly	Mood ≥ 20
		Daily ≥ 10

CATEGORY	INTERACTION	RECIPIENT REQUIREMENTS
Insult		Daily ≥ 25
Play	Rough House	Mood ≥ 20
Scold		Mood ≥ -25
Tease	Scare	Mood between -10 and 15
	Taunt	Daily ≥ 10
Tickle		Mood ≥ 15, Playful ≥ 1

Adult-to-Child Interaction Results

INTERACTION	RESPONSE	DAILY RELATIONSHIP CHANGE	LIFETIME RELATIONSHIP CHANGE	SOCIAL SCORE CHANGE
Brag	Accept	5	0	10
	Reject	-5	-1	0
Be Bragged To	Accept	3	0	5
	Reject	-5	-1	0
Cheer Up	Accept	5	0	7
	Reject	-3	0	0
Be Cheered Up	Accept	10	2	7
	Reject	-10	-2	0
Entertain—Joke	Accept	3	1	9
	Reject	-6	0	0
Be Entertained—Joke	Accept	4	2	10
	Reject	-7	0	0
Entertain—Juggle	Accept	3	1	7
	Reject	-10	-2	0
Be Entertained—Juggle	Accept	4	2	10
	Reject	-7	-1	0
Hug—Nice	Accept	4	1	8
	Reject	-5	-1	0
Be Hugged—Nice	Accept	4	1	8
	Reject	-5	-1	0

Adult-to-Child Interaction Results, continued

INTERACTION	RESPONSE	DAILY RELATIONSHIP CHANGE	LIFETIME RELATIONSHIP CHANGE	SOCIAL SCORE CHANGE
Hug—Friendly	Accept	5	2	10
	Reject	-10	-3	0
Be Hugged—Friendly	Accept	5	2	10
	Reject	-10	-2	-2
Insult	Accept	-10	-1	5
	Reject	-6	-3	0
Be Insulted	Accept	-14	-3	-7
	Reject	-12	-5	-10
Play—Rough House	Accept	3	1	9
	Reject	-6	0	0
Be Played With— Rough House	Accept	4	2	10
	Reject	-7	0	0
Scold	Accept	5	3	5
	Reject	-8	-3	2
Be Scolded	Accept	5	3	10
	Reject	-10	-2	-2
Tease—Scare	Accept	5	1	10
	Reject	-5	-1	0
Be Teased—Scare	Accept	5	1	8
	Reject	-10	-2	0
Tease—Taunt	Accept	4	0	7
	Reject	-3	0	-3
Be Teased—Taunt	Accept	4	1	7
	Reject	-10	-1	-7
Tickle	Accept	8	1	10
	Reject	-5	-1	0
Be Tickled	Accept	5	1	10
	Reject	-8	-2	0

Adult-to-Child Interaction Menu Triggers

CATEGORY	INTERACTION	INITIATOR REQUIREMENTS	RECIPIENT REQUIREMENTS
Brag		Mood < 10, Daily ≥ 10, Daily ≤ 50	None
Cheer Up		Mood ≥ 25, Daily ≥ 25	Mood ≤ 0
Entertain	Joke	Playful ≥ 4, Mood ≥ 40	None
		Mood > 50	None
	Juggle	Playful ≥ 5, Mood ≥ 40	None
		Mood ≥ 50	None
Hug	Nice	Daily ≥ 30, Mood > 30	None
	Friendly	Daily ≥ 35, Mood > 35	None
Insult		Mood ≤ -10	None

Adult-to-Child Interaction Menu Triggers, continued

CATEGORY	INTERACTION	INITIATOR REQUIREMENTS	RECIPIENT REQUIREMENTS
Play	Rough House	Playful ≥ 4, Mood ≥ 20	None
		Mood ≥ 40	None
Scold		None	Mood ≤ -10
Tease	Scare	Mood ≤ 5	None
		Daily ≤ -5	None
	Taunt	Mood ≤ 15	None
		Daily ≤ -5	None
Tickle		Playful ≥ 2, Mood ≥ 0	None
		Mood > 30	None

Child-to-Adult Interactions

Child-to-Adult Interaction Menu Triggers

CATEGORY	INTERACTION	INITIATOR REQUIREMENTS	RECIPIENT REQUIREMENTS
Brag		Daily ≥ 10, Mood ≥ 20	None
Cheer Up		Daily ≥ 5, Mood ≥ 0	Mood ≤ 0
Entertain	Crazy Dance	None	Social ≤ 50
	Handstand	None	Social ≤ 30
	Joke	Mood ≥ 0	None
	Perform Trick	Mood ≥ 10	None
Hug	Nice	Mood ≥ 30, Daily ≥ 30	None
	Friendly	Mood ≥ 35, Daily ≥ 35	None
Insult		Mood ≥ -10, Daily ≥ -5	None
Play	Rock-Paper-Scissors	Mood ≥ 50	None
Talk	Jabber	Daily ≥ 10	None
Tease	Scare	Daily < 10, Mood ≤ -10	None
	Taunt	Daily < 15, Mood ≤ -15	None
Tickle		Mood > 5	None

Child-to-Adult Interaction Results

INTERACTION	RESPONSE	DAILY RELATIONSHIP CHANGE	LIFETIME RELATIONSHIP CHANGE	SOCIAL SCORE CHANGE
Brag	Accept	5	0	10
	Reject	-5	-1	0
Be Bragged To	Accept	3	0	5
	Reject	-5	-1	0
Cheer Up	Accept	5	0	7
	Reject	-3	0	0
Be Cheered Up	Accept	10	2	7
	Reject	-10	-2	0
Entertain—Joke	Accept	3	1	9
	Reject	-6	0	0

...ild-to-Adult Interaction Results, continued

INTERACTION	RESPONSE	DAILY RELATIONSHIP CHANGE	LIFETIME RELATIONSHIP CHANGE	SOCIAL SCORE CHANGE
Be Entertained—Joke	Accept	4	2	10
	Reject	-7	0	0
Entertain—Perform Trick	Accept	3	1	7
	Reject	-5	-1	0
Be Entertained—Perform Trick	Accept	4	2	10
	Reject	-7	-1	0
Entertain—Crazy Dance	Accept	4	2	6
	Reject	-6	-1	0
Be Entertained—Crazy Dance	Accept	3	1	5
	Reject	-5	0	0
Hug—Nice	Accept	4	1	8
	Reject	-5	-1	0
Be Hugged—Nice	Accept	4	1	8
	Reject	-5	-1	0
Hug—Friendly	Accept	5	2	10
	Reject	-10	-3	0
Be Hugged—Friendly	Accept	5	2	10
	Reject	-10	-2	-2
Insult	Accept	-10	-1	5
	Reject	-6	-3	0
Be Insulted	Accept	-14	-3	-7
	Reject	-12	-5	-10
Play—Rock-Paper-Scissors	Accept	5	1	6
	Reject	-5	-1	-2
Be Played With—Rock-Paper-Scissors	Accept	7	2	6
	Reject	-9	-3	-2
Talk—Jabber	Accept	4	1	5
	Reject	-4	-2	-1
Hear Talk—Jabber	Accept	4	0	5
	Reject	-3	0	0
Tease—Scare	Accept	5	1	10
	Reject	-5	-1	0
Be Teased—Scare	Accept	5	1	8
	Reject	-10	-2	0
Tease—Taunt	Accept	4	0	7
	Reject	-3	0	-3
Be Teased—Taunt	Accept	4	1	7
	Reject	-10	-1	-7
Tickle	Accept	8	1	10
	Reject	-5	-1	0
Tickled	Accept	5	1	10
	Reject	-8	-2	0

Child-to-Adult Interaction Success Requirements

CATEGORY	INTERACTION	INITIATOR REQUIREMENTS	RECIPIENT REQUIREMENTS
Brag		Mood ≥ 20, Daily ≥ 10	None
Cheer Up		Mood ≥ 0, Daily ≥ 5	Mood ≤ 0
Entertain	Crazy Dance	None	Social ≤ 0
	Handstand	None	Social ≤ 0
	Joke	Mood ≥ 0	None
Hug	Nice	Daily ≥ 30, Mood > 30	None
	Friendly	Daily ≥ 35, Mood > 35	None
Insult		Mood ≤ -10	None
		Daily ≤ -5	None
Play	Rock-Paper-Scissors	Mood ≥ 50	None
Talk	Jabber	Daily ≥ 10	None
Tease	Scare	Mood ≤ 10	None
		Daily ≤ 10	None
	Taunt	Mood ≤ 15	None
		Daily ≤ 15	None
Tickle		Mood ≥ 5	None

Child-to-Child Interactions

Child-to-Child Interaction Success Requirements

CATEGORY	INTERACTION	RECIPIENT REQUIREMENTS
Annoy	Poke	Mood ≥ 0, Daily ≥ 15
	Push	Mood ≥ 0, Daily ≥ 10
	Kick Shin	Mood ≥ 0, Daily ≥ 5
Brag		Daily ≥ 20
Cheer Up		Daily ≥ 20
Entertain	Joke	Mood ≥ 20, Daily > -25
	Perform Trick	Mood ≥ 15, Daily > -15
Hug	Nice	Mood ≥ 20, Daily ≥ 10
	Friendly	Mood ≥ 20, Daily ≥ 10
Insult		Mood > 0, Daily > 20
Play	Rock-Paper-Scissors	Mood ≥ 15
	Tag	Mood ≥ 15
Talk	Jabber	Mood ≥ 20, Social ≤ 5
	Whisper	No Data
Tease	Scare	Daily ≥ 30
	Taunt	Daily > 10
		Nice > 3
Tickle		Mood ≥ 25, Daily ≥ 30

...d-to-Child Interaction Results

...ERACTION	RESPONSE	DAILY RELATIONSHIP CHANGE	LIFETIME RELATIONSHIP CHANGE	SOCIAL SCORE CHANGE
...noy—Push	Accept	-6	-1	6
	Reject	-6	-2	1
Annoyed—Push	Accept	-3	-1	6
	Reject	-7	-3	-1
...noy—Poke	Accept	-4	0	7
	Reject	-4	-1	0
Annoyed—Poke	Accept	-2	0	3
	Reject	-5	-1	0
...noy—Kick Shin	Accept	-8	-2	10
	Reject	-8	-5	2
Annoyed—Kick Shin	Accept	-6	-2	9
	Reject	-10	-8	-2
...g	Accept	5	0	10
	Reject	-5	-1	0
Bragged To	Accept	3	0	5
	Reject	-5	-1	0
...eer Up	Accept	5	0	7
	Reject	-3	0	0
Cheered Up	Accept	10	2	7
	Reject	-10	-2	0
...tertain—Joke	Accept	3	1	9
	Reject	-6	0	0
Entertained—Joke	Accept	4	2	10
	Reject	-7	0	0
...tertain—Perform Trick	Accept	3	1	7
	Reject	-10	-2	0
Entertained—Perform ...k	Accept	4	2	10
	Reject	-7	-1	0
...g—Nice	Accept	4	1	8
	Reject	-5	-1	0
Hugged—Nice	Accept	4	1	8
	Reject	-5	-1	0
...g—Friendly	Accept	5	2	10
	Reject	-10	-3	0
Hugged—Friendly	Accept	5	2	10
	Reject	-10	-2	-2
...ult	Accept	-10	-1	5
	Reject	-6	-3	0
Insulted	Accept	-14	-3	-7
	Reject	-12	-5	-10

Child-to-Child Interaction Results

INTERACTION	RESPONSE	DAILY RELATIONSHIP CHANGE	LIFETIME RELATIONSHIP CHANGE	SOCIAL SCORE CHANGE
Play—Rock-Paper-Scissors	Accept	5	1	6
	Reject	-2	-1	0
Be Played With—Rock-Paper-Scissors	Accept	7	2	6
	Reject	-9	-3	-2
Play—Tag	Accept	No Data		
	Reject	No Data		
Be Played With—Tag	Accept	No Data		
	Reject	No Data		
Talk—Jabber	Accept	4	1	5
	Reject	-4	-1	-1
Hear Talk—Jabber	Accept	4	0	5
	Reject	-3	0	0
Tease—Scare	Accept	5	1	10
	Reject	-3	0	0
Be Teased—Scare	Accept	5	1	8
	Reject	-10	1	0
Tease—Taunt	Accept	4	0	7
	Reject	-5	-1	-3
Be Teased—Taunt	Accept	4	1	7
	Reject	-10	2	-7
Tickle	Accept	8	1	10
	Reject	-5	-1	0
Be Tickled	Accept	5	1	10
	Reject	-8	-2	0

Child-to-Child Interaction Menu Triggers

CATEGORY	INTERACTION	INITIATOR REQUIREMENTS	RECIPIENT REQUIREMENTS
Annoy	Poke	Mood ≤ -20	None
	Push	Mood ≤ -10	None
	Kick Shin	Mood ≤ -30	None
Brag		Daily ≥ 10, Mood ≤ 20	None
Cheer Up		Mood ≥ 0	Mood ≤ 0
Entertain	Joke	Mood ≥ 25	None
	Perform Trick	Mood ≥ 25	None
Hug	Nice	Mood ≥ 30, Daily ≥ 30	None
	Friendly	Mood ≥ 35, Daily ≥ 35	None
Insult		Mood ≤ 0	None
		Daily ≤ -10	None
Play	Rock-Paper-Scissors	Mood ≥ 50, Daily ≥ 25	None
	Tag	Mood ≥ 0, Daily ≥ 30	None

d-to-Child Interaction Menu Triggers, continued

TEGORY	INTERACTION	INITIATOR REQUIREMENTS	RECIPIENT REQUIREMENTS
lk	Jabber	Daily ≥ 10	None
	Whisper	Mood ≥ 15, Daily ≥ 15	None
ase	Scare	Mood ≥ 20	None
		Daily > 0	None
	Taunt	Mood ≤ 15	None
		Daily > 15	None
:kle		Mood ≥ 5	None

s SUPERSTAR Social Interaction Requirements

Peer Levels

Key			FAME LEVEL	PEER RANGE	WIDENET PEER RANGE
A	Initiator		0 or 1	0-3	0-5
3	Recipient		2	0-4	0-6
TR	Long Term Relationship		3	1-5	0-6
TR	Short Term Relationship		4	2-5	1-7
>	Greater than		5	3-6	2-7
<	Less than		6	3-7	2-8
			7	4-9	4-10
			8	6-9	5-10
			9	7-10	5-10
			10	8-10	6-10

e Socials (FameA > 0)

:IAL INTERACTION	MENU TRIGGER	ACCEPT/REJECT REQUIREMENTS
eet: Wave	FameA > 0	If FameA > FameB, STR > -10 OR If NiceB > 8, STR > -20 OR If FameB < 50, STR > -10, If FameA < 20 Accept; All else reject
eet: Shake Hands	FameA > 0	If FameA > FameB, STR > -30 OR If STR > -40 accept; If NiceB < 3 reject; All else reject
eet: Star Kiss	FameA > 0	If FameA > 15, STR > -40 accept; All else reject
ve: Autograph	FameA > 3, MoodA > -30	If FameA > FameB, FameA > 23, A/B fame NOT A PEER, STR between -10 and 35, LTR < 40 OR
		If FameA > 5, Creativity > 8, Charisma > 5, MoodB > 0, FameB < 100 OR
		If FameA > 10, Creativity > 9, Charisma > 9, MoodB > 20 then accept autograph; All else reject (crumple) autograph

Fame Socials (FameA > 0), continued

SOCIAL INTERACTION	MENU TRIGGER	ACCEPT/REJECT REQUIREMENTS
Talk: About Self	FameA > 3, MoodA > -10	If FameA > FameB, OR If A/B Fame is PEER, MoodB > -20 OR If CharismaA > 8, OR If A/B Fame is WIDENET PEER, SimA = HighFashion then accept; All else reject (act bored)
Brag: About Starpower	FameA > 3	If FameA > FameB, STR is 0-25, A/B Fame is NOT A PEER OR If FameA > FameB, CharismaA > 8, HygieneA > 0, OR If A/B Fame = PEER, HygieneA > 0, SimA = High Fashion, Charisma > 3. then accept; All else reject
Talk: About Biz	FameA > 5, MoodA > -20	If A/B Fame WIDENET PEER and MoodB > -40, OR If FameA > FameB OR If STR > 30, MoodB > -20 then accept; All else reject (bored)

Fan Socials (FameA < FameB)

SOCIAL INTERACTION	MENU TRIGGER	ACCEPT/REJECT REQUIREMENTS
Compliment: I'm Your Biggest Fan!	FameA < FameB, MoodA > -20, FameB > 30	MoodB.0, STR < 30, FameA < 55 OR MoodB > -40,STR < 30, NiceB > 8, FameA < 30, then accept (compliment, freak out); All else reject (brush away)
Ask: For Autograph?	FameA < FameB, MoodA > -10, BFame > 23	If MoodB > -20, STR < 30 then accept All else reject (brush away)
Ask: Can I Hug You?	FameA < FameB, MoodA > 0, FameB > 30	If MoodB > 20, OutgoingB > 4, STRB > HygieneA > -10, OR BodyA > 4, MoodB > 0, HygieneA > -10, then accept; All else reject (brush away)
Compliment: I'm not worthy	FameA < FameB, MoodA < 0	If MoodB > 40; All else reject

Socials (FameA = FameB, see Peer Level table)

AL INTERACTION	MENU TRIGGER	ACCEPT/REJECT REQUIREMENTS
k: Stage Photo Op?	FameA > 25, FameB > 25, MoodA > 0	If MoodB > -40, STRB > 15, A/B Fame WIDENET PEER, A = High Fashion, OR If MoodB > -40, STRB > 15, A/B Fame PEER, then accept (good photo); All else reject (talk to the hand)
: Stage Publicity Event?	FameA > 25, FameB > 25, A/B Fame PEER, MoodA > 0	MoodB > -10, STR > 25 opposite gender, then accept (Big Kiss) OR MoodB > -10, STR > 25 same gender, then accept (Mock Fight) OR MoodB < -20, then Mega-reject (Push Fight), STR < -20, then Mega-reject (Push Fight); All else reject (Talk to the hand)
npliment: Star Quality	FameA > 5, FameB > 5, FameA < FameB, MoodA > -5	A/B Fame = PEER, MoodB > -30 OR A/B Fame = WIDENET PEER, MoodB > 0 OR A/B Fame = NOT A PEER, STR 25, then accept (Do you really think so?); All else reject (Are you talking to me? and Shoo!)
k: Weren't You in the Tabloid?	MoodA > -70, FameB > 0	If MoodB > -40, STR between -10 and 35, LTR < 40, AFame > = Bfame, then Accept (Talk); If MoodB > -40, STR between -10 and 35, LTR < 40, AFame < BFame then Accept (Brag/Boast); If FameA < FameB and A/B Fame > 400, Reject (Don't you know who I am? and Shoo!); All else reject

rity Socials (FameA > FameB)

AL INTERACTION	MENU TRIGGER	ACCEPT/REJECT REQUIREMENTS
e: Kiss	FameA > FameB, MoodA > 20, OutgoingA >	If A/B Fame = NOT A PEER, FameB < 50, MoodB > -5 OR PlayfulB < 8, MoodB > -10, then accept (star struck kiss); If HygieneA < -20, reject; All else reject (push away)
k: Were you admiring me?	FameA > 5, MoodA > -30	FameA > FameB, FameB < 50, A/B Fame = NOT A PEER, STR between -10 and 35, LTR < 40, MoodB > -30 OR A/B Fame = PEER, PlayfulB > 7, MoodB > 0 OR A/B Fame = PEER and BodyA > 8 OR A/B Fame = PEER and CharismaA > 8; If A/B Fame = PEER, SimA = HighFashion, OR OutgoingB > 4, then accept (Coy Giggle); All else reject (Slap)

Sims Superstar Social Interactions

NOTE The Fame Change values noted in the following table reflect the behind-the-scenes compilation of points that determines when a player reaches the Fame requirement for promotion or demotion. The value changes listed below are not immediately visible in the game, unless the change is enough to push a player up or down to the next level (if all other requirements are met).

Superstar Socials: Initiator

INTERACTION	RESPONSE	FAME CHANGE	SOCIAL MOTIVE CHANGE	DAILY RELATIONSHIP CHANGE
I'm your biggest fan!	Accept	0	7	6
	Reject	0	1	-2
Ask for autograph	Accept	0	6	4
	Reject	0	1	-1
Ask for hug	Accept	0	6	4
	Reject	0	1	-1
Stage Photo Op?	Accept	4	5	5
	Reject	0	0	-2
Stage Publicity Event?	Accept	5	7	5
	Reject	0	0	-2
Were you in tabloid?	Accept	0	5	3
	Reject	0	0	-2
Compliment Starpower	Accept	0	5	5
	Reject	0	0	-5
Talk about self	Accept	1	10	7
	Reject	0	0	-5
Give autograph	Accept	1	5	2
	Reject	0	0	-3
Talk about Biz	Accept	0	6	5
	Reject	0	0	-2
Give Star kiss	Accept	0	2	2
	Reject	0	0	-4

tar Socials: Initiator, continued

ACTION	RESPONSE	FAME CHANGE	SOCIAL MOTIVE CHANGE	DAILY RELATIONSHIP CHANGE
e you admiring me?	Accept	0	2	2
	Reject	0	0	-2
ot worthy	Accept	0	6	6
	Reject	0	1	-2
about Starpower	Accept	0	4	3
	Reject	-10	0	-5
air kiss	Accept	0	1	1
	Reject	0	-1	-1
t with shake hands	Accept	0	1	1
	Reject	0	-1	-1
t with wave	Accept	0	1	1
	Reject	0	-1	-1

star Socials: Receiver

ACTION	RESPONSE	FAME CHANGE	SOCIAL MOTIVE CHANGE	DAILY RELATIONSHIP CHANGE
our biggest fan!	Accept	1	4	4
	Reject	-1	1	-2
or autograph	Accept	1	2	1
	Reject	-1	1	-1
or hug	Accept	1	4	3
	Reject	0	1	-1
e Photo Op?	Accept	4	5	3
	Reject	-4	0	-2
e Publicity Event?	Accept	5	7	5
	Reject	0	0	-2
e you in tabloid?	Accept	0	5	3
	Reject	0	0	-2
pliment Starpower	Accept	0	17	5
	Reject	0	0	-5

Superstar Socials: Receiver, continued

INTERACTION	RESPONSE	FAME CHANGE	SOCIAL MOTIVE CHANGE	DAILY RELATIONSHIP CHANGE
Talk about self	Accept	0	5	3
	Reject	0	0	-7
Give autograph	Accept	0	5	10
	Reject	0	0	-3
Talk about Biz	Accept	0	6	5
	Reject	0	0	-2
Give Star kiss	Accept	0	2	2
	Reject	0	0	-4
Were you admiring me?	Accept	0	2	2
	Reject	0	0	-2
I'm not worthy	Accept	0	6	1
	Reject	0	1	-4
Brag about Starpower	Accept	0	4	3
	Reject	-10	0	-5
Give air kiss	Accept	0	1	1
	Reject	0	-1	-1
Greet with shake hands	Accept	0	1	1
	Reject	0	-1	-1
Greet with wave	Accept	0	1	1
	Reject	0	-1	-1